Illustrated

BSA Buyer's Guide™

Model-by-model analysis of postwar singles, twins, triples and specials

Roy Bacon

Niton Publishing

Published in 1990 by Niton Publishing, PO Box 3, Ventor, Isle of Wight PO38 2AS England

British Library Cataloguing in Publication Data
Bacon, Roy H. (Roy Hunt)
    Illustrated BSA motorcycle buyer's guide.
    1. BSA motorcycles, history
    I. Title
629.2'275
ISBN 0-9514204-1-0

On the front cover: This 1963 Rocket Gold Star was found in poor condition in 1985 and stored until late 1987. Its restoration was then undertaken by owner Don Harrell at his motorcycle shop in Visalia, California, and completed by April 1988. His high standards are clear from the picture and it's no wonder that the machine soon won many show awards. *Carol McGrew*

On the back cover: Two pinnacles of the BSA marque, the Clubman Gold Star DB32 350 cc, with its twittering silencer, and the Rocket 3 750 cc triple, with its "ray gun" silencers, here of 1970 vintage.

Printed and bound in the United States of America

Contents

Acknowledgements

This is the second in this series written under the Niton Publishing imprint and takes its place alongside others published by Motorbooks International in the USA and Aston Publications in the UK. In this way the three houses have combined to produce a range of *Illustrated Buyer's Guides* covering machines from both sides of the Atlantic.

As with the *Illustrated Triumph Buyer's Guide*, I have been helped and supported by Tim Parker and his editorial team at Motorbooks who took on the task of guiding me into the world of book production. My thanks go to all who assisted along the way.

Once again I turned to the magazines for the pictures and have to thank Malcolm Gough, editor of *Motor Cycle News*, and EMAP, whose archives hold the old *Motor Cycle Weekly* files, for the bulk of them. Others came from the Mick Woollett archive and some I took myself, mainly at shows or museums, as will be clear from their background.

The front cover picture was taken by Carol McGrew in California and features a lovely Rocket Gold Star after its restoration by Don Harrell. Don was kind enough to send me the picture when the machine was rebuilt and later, at my request, sent the transparency to Motorbooks for the cover to be prepared.

Few of the photographs carried the imprint of a professional due to the way they reached me but one that did was taken by Cecil Bailey and is of his inevitable high standard. All borrowed photographs were returned to their source following publication and I have tried to make contact to clear copyright. If my letter failed to reach you or I have used an unmarked print without realising this, I can only apologise.

Finally my thanks to the professionals of the printing and book binding industry who helped me bring my second imprint to completion.

Introduction

The *Illustrated BSA Buyer's Guide* covers all the postwar production motorcycles, scooters, cyclemotors and mopeds of the Small Heath firm that played such a great role in the history of the British motorcycle industry. It may have ended in tears and aggravation, but along the way the firm built some nice motorcycles and enjoyed considerable competition success.

BSA was not known for radical advances but built good, solid and reliable machines which it backed up with an exceptional spares network. Its prices were always affordable and thus its machines sold in large numbers to all types of owners across the globe.

When interest in older machines rose in the 1980s the marque was again in the forefront. This was partly because of the sheer numbers of machines still available or stored in the backs of sheds and garages. Coupled with this was a good stock of spares plus plenty of information in the form of manuals and spares lists, so work on most models was relatively easy.

Lovely CB Gold Star in road trim, something not often seen. The spare magneto they are holding must be a bonus—pure enthusiasm for a fine hobby and machine.

The 654 cc Lightning Clubman raced by the great Mike Hailwood in the production race at Silverstone in 1965. He won as usual, and also took two other events.

In addition, many past owners returned to motorcycling with a BSA because they knew the marque from past experience. Younger classic machine enthusiasts were often steered to BSA by older friends or relations, or because the models were a good starting point for a first restoration and easy to come by.

All this brings many benefits but there are also areas to beware of, as not all machines are what they claim to be. For instance, any Bantam engine can fit any Bantam frame, so changes are common although the electrics can be a problem in some cases. Gold Stars, B or M range singles and the twins often shared cycle parts as well. So, all that glistens is not Gold.

It is all too easy, in many cases, to switch parts from one range to another and produce a machine that, on the surface, can claim a fine pedigree. All too often that Rocket Gold Star turns out to have a B31 frame and iron A10 engine, along with an assortment of details from a variety of sources.

This book is designed to help you detect these hybrids so that you really do know what you are putting your money down for. There is no reason *not* to run a hybrid, but only as long as it is in safe condition, you know what it is built up from, you are happy with the specification and the price paid reflects all of this.

Your best weapons when buying are knowledge and detailed information on engine and frame numbers, colours and other identity details found in the appendices. These, and other aspects of buying, are covered more in the last chapter, but first you need to learn about BSA models. With data of what was built and when, you can be confident of finding the good buys and avoiding the trouble spots.

Each chapter looks at a series or a model type from the BSA range and includes an investment rating using stars from one to five. These are at best an educated guess based on 1989 conditions so could be entirely wrong. Therefore there is no guarantee given or implied, for there are bound to be a couple of jokers in the pack. At the turn of the century we can look back with twenty-twenty hindsight and see what they were.

Before buying, always check out current prices for your part of the world as these can be altered by local events as well as general trends. Few realised the way prices would move in the 1980s and no one knows what the pattern will be over the next decade.

For the really dedicated BSA man, the right number plate, illuminated sign on the roof and star badge sticker on the windscreen!

Investment rating

The investment rating system works as follows:

★★★★★ Five are the tops, the highest priced and usually have the best chance of appreciating. They are most likely to be sold by contacts and word of mouth, sometimes at auctions or more expensively by a specialist dealer.

★★★★ Four are the best that most people can acquire, as there are not enough five-star machines to go round. Still they are desirable and worth having from all points of view. If advertised, check with care; one in poor condition will cost to get into true four-star condition.

★★★ Three are the middle-of-the-road, nice machines that hold their price along with market trends. Most machines in daily use come from this class, where good condition and reliability are the norm but must be checked for.

★★ Two are less desirable and less able to keep their value up with the market, but can still be nice machines if they are what you want.

★ One are the machines few want, are nonoriginal or need too much work to be true. They can be a longshot, although this is unlikely now, but as always, if it is the one you want then you can probably buy it cheaply. If it is not, then leave it alone.

In addition to the investment rating, a buyer must consider the three Cs—complete, correct and condition. All have a major effect on the price of the machine but not on its ultimate star rating. First, being complete is important for a machine bought for restoration. It is the small details that demand more attention than the large, for there are many involved in the build-up of a machine. Finding all the missing ones can be expensive and time consuming.

Second, correct parts are important for a restoration, although less so for a machine being built for daily use. The reverse applies to the third factor, condition. For the restorer is mainly concerned with having correct parts regardless, more or less, of their condition. If the machine is to be used for daily riding, then the rider wants top condition whether the part is correct or a modern equivalent.

As always, you make your decision, pay your money and make your choice. Whatever it is, I hope it brings you good riding and much enjoyment—which just might be better than buying that five-star investment you dare not take out on the road.

Chapter 1

Bantam

★★★/★★	D1, rigid, Wipac	1948–55
★★★	D1, rigid, Lucas	1950–53
★★/★	D1, plunger, Wipac	1950–63
★★★	D1, plunger, Lucas	1950–53
★★★	D1, competition, rigid	1950–55
★★★	D1, competition, Lucas	1950–53
★★★	D1, competition, plunger	1950–54
★★★	D1, competition, plunger, Lucas	1950–53
★★	D1, battery	1954–55
★★/★	D1, plunger, battery	1954–63
★★	D3, plunger	1954–55
★★	D3, plunger, battery	1954–55
★★★	D3, competition	1954–55
★★★	D3, competition, plunger	1954
★★	D3, swing arm	1956–57
★★	D3, swing arm, battery	1956–57
★★★	D5, direct	1958
★★★	D5, battery	1958
★	D7 Super	1959–65
★	D7 Super de luxe	1964–65
★★	D7 Silver	1966
★★	D7 de luxe	1966
★	D10 Silver	1966–67
★	D10 Supreme	1966–67
★★	D10 Sports	1966–67
★★★	D10 Bushman	1966–67
★	D14/4 Supreme	1968
★★	D14/4S Sports	1968
★★★	D14/4B Bushman	1968
★	D175	1969–71
★★	D175B Bushman	1969–70

The BSA Bantam made its debut as an engine unit in March 1948, with the complete machine appearing in June as the export-only D1 model. It became one of the most successful machines ever made in England and remained in production in some form until 1971.

The Bantam was, however, not an English design but based on the prewar German DKW RT125, which was taken over as part of the war reparations. In time that design was also used by Harley-Davidson, Yamaha, the Polish WSK and the Russian Voskhod while DKW continued with it in the postwar years. It was also used by MZ which was based in the old DKW factory in East Germany.

Bantam

BSA reversed the design to create a mirror image with the gear and kickstart pedals on the right while also changing to English electrics. Otherwise it kept much to the original including the outline of the head and barrel, but did convert the dimensions to inches for all details.

The engine was based on a 58 mm stroke, which was to be common for all Bantams, and the D1 had a 52 mm bore and thus was of 123 cc. It was built in-unit with a three-speed gearbox and was a conventional two-stroke, which was well up to date when launched but gradually fell behind the times.

The crankcase extended back to include the gearbox and was split vertically on the cylinder centre line. It was cast in light alloy with a spigot bore for the cylinder and a location diameter and recess around the flywheels. In addition, there were hollow dowels in the top front and rear engine mountings to hold the cases in alignment. In practice, the cases were best set so the barrel mounting face was dead flat and the dowels then driven in.

The pressed-up crankshaft had full flywheels that were larger than really necessary which, in turn, increased the height of

Engine of the first 1948 Bantam with its Wipac generator. The top generator outlet was prone to let water in and was soon changed. The first of a long line of machines.

the engine. The wheels were not solid but forged, with the balance weight form within the outer circle which was then sealed by a steel disk held in a recess by staking. These disks are known to come loose and will then continue spinning when the engine stops running.

Both mainshafts were press fit into the flywheels, as was the shouldered crankpin. The big end was a single row of uncaged rollers which ran directly in the connecting rod eye. The rod itself was a steel stamping with a bushed small end for the hollow gudgeon pin, retained by wire circlips in the piston.

Competition version of the D1 Bantam as prepared for the International Six Days Trial and little altered from standard. Nice and light to paddle up the hills.

The alloy piston had a small dome to the crown and two plain rings, pegged to prevent their rotation. On each side below the gudgeon pin there were cut-outs to allow the mixture to flow into the transfer ports; the piston was quite short by English standards of the time. It ran in a cast-iron cylinder that inclined forward a little and had an inlet stub to the rear, angled to be horizontal. There were two transfer ports, with one on each side to match passages cast in the crankcase, and the ports directed the gas flow to the back wall of the cylinder. A single central exhaust in the cylinder fed a port offset to the right for the outlet which was threaded externally for the pipe nut.

A light alloy cylinder head went on top of the barrel to give a compression ratio of 6.5:1, and its fins were styled to match those on the cylinder. The combustion chamber was part spherical with the sparking plug laid well back at an angle on the centre line. Both head and barrel were held by nuts on four long studs screwed into the crankcase. There was no head gasket.

The crankshaft turned in three ball race main bearings with one on the left with an oil seal outboard of it. The other two mains went on the right with a seal between them, and the inner races were lubricated by oil holes drilled down from the transfer passages. The outer main on the right was lubricated by the transmission oil while the rest of the engine relied on petroil, with the big end fed via slots cut in the rod eye.

A Wipac flywheel magneto and generator went on the left end of the crankshaft with the stator outboard of the rotor. The rotor was keyed to a tapered part of the shaft and enclosed by a casting which extended back to house the clutch lift mechanism. It carried the stator, with its ignition and lighting coils, plus the contact points whose cam went on the extreme end of the crankshaft. A bronze bush in the stator plate acted as an outer main bearing but had little chance of keeping the long, whippy shaft and heavy rotor under much control.

The points went under a small cover, while the high-tension lead connected via an adaptor held in the top of the stator. The ignition timing was set by moving the stator

BSA Bantam Major 150 c.c. Model D 3

By 1954 the Bantam was also listed as the 148 cc D3. A plunger frame was available for either engine size. It could also have battery lighting and had lost the early type silencer.

ing in slots, and the poor fit of stator to casting was often an asset. It allowed the bronze bush to take up a natural position on the mainshaft, and by moving the stator about the lighting output could be varied.

The primary drive went on the right with a single strand chain connecting the engine and clutch sprockets. The clutch had three plates with cork inserts and six, nonadjustable springs. It was held together with one large circlip, ran on a bronze flanged bush and was very tough. The quick-thread lift mechanism with central adjustment screw went on the left and moved the clutch pressure plate via a pushrod and separate mushroom. These went in the gearbox mainshaft, on which the clutch was fitted, and the operating cable swept in under the magneto housing to a cast-in socket.

The clutch drove a cross-over gearbox with the layshaft positioned below the mainshaft and the change mechanism to the rear. The shafts ran in bushes, with a ball race for the clutch end of the mainshaft and the sleeve gear which had an oil seal outboard of the race and bushes in its bore. The final-drive sprocket was on the left with the clutch lift mechanism and casting outboard of it.

The two middle gears moved together under the control of a simple plate, which indexed their positions, and a positive stop mechanism. This had the gear pedal on the right with an up-for-up movement, while the mechanism included a small pointer on the left to indicate which gear was engaged.

The gearbox worked well, although the index notch for second gear was not deep enough in early engines and the pedal return spring was inside the crankcase. Thus, when it broke, the cases had to be split in order to replace it. In addition, the jump from second to top was large, so most owners ran up to peak speed before changing and occasionally would forget which way the pedal moved. If they went into bottom by mistake, the change could be traumatic and a quick way of stripping the mainshaft gear of its teeth.

Later came both close and wide ratio boxes, although neither were ever fitted as

For 1956 the D3 went into a pivoted-fork frame although the D1 stayed with its plungers to the end. There was also a longer silencer but the engine was much the same.

rare but a definite asset for road use, especially if the engine is tuned as well.

The gear pedal shaft ran through the centre of the kickstart one which turned in the outer chaincase. The kickstart carried a quadrant that meshed with a gear run on the back of the clutch, with a spring ratchet for its return. This gave primary kickstarting, handy to the novice rider and nearly unique for a British machine at that time. A clock spring returned the kickstart and could be changed once the cover was removed, this being held by five screws.

The primary drive and gearbox shared the same oil so there were passages between the two chambers. There was only one small, angled filler in the top of the crankcase, and one drain plug, plus one for the crankcase; the filler plug had a dipstick attached to it.

This engine unit, first offered by itself, went into a simple welded loop frame. The mounting plates at front and rear picked up with the four fixings in the crankcase, and other lugs carried the tank, seat, toolbox, chainguard, mudguard and footrest bar. This last had both the centre stand and the rear

plate which was held by three screws work-standard, and by selection a much better set of ratios could be arrived at. These boxes are

The next step was to 172 cc and the 1958 D5 which had a new flange-mounted carburettor but the same frame and forks as had been used by the D3.

The D7 replaced the D5 for 1959 and had a much longer run in its new frame with nacelle forks but the same 172 cc engine plus a cover for the generator.

brake pedal pivoted on it with the stand held up by a spring clip.

At the front were simple telescopic forks with internal springs and grease lubrication but no damping. The speedometer went on the pressed top yoke and the headlamp hung from a bracket bolted to the bottom one. The bulb horn was fitted into the steering stem with the bulb screwed into the top and the outlet at the bottom. Split clamps for the handlebar fixed them to the top yoke, and the control lever pivots were welded into place.

Both wheels had offset hubs with 5 in. single leading shoe drum brakes and steel rims with 2.75x19 in. tyres. The front was shielded by a deeply valanced sprung mudguard which carried the number plate on each side. The rear mudguard had a valance that varied in depth, and one of its supports was a rear carrier.

The toolbox hung from a frame lug under the saddle and bolted to the top rear engine mounting just behind the small Amal carburettor, with air cleaner which clipped to the cylinder stub. The exhaust pipe ran down on the right to a thin silencer that became known as the "flat Bantam" type. The fuel tank was formed from pressings welded together, with the seams running the length of the tank top as a styling feature.

Direct lighting was used but the control was a handlebar-mounted lever on the left which connected to the alloy headlamp with a cable. The switch itself was housed in the shell which also carried a small dry battery for the pilot lamp. The machine finish was mist green with yellow tank panels, and the chrome plating was restricted to the exhaust system and handlebars.

In this form the Bantam went on sale and proved popular all over the world. Problem areas were weak electrics and centre stand, and the high position of both gear and brake pedals were a nuisance. But the machine was tough and stood up well to the punishment novice riders handed out. It could run up to nearly 50 mph, handled nicely, had excellent brakes and was comfortable, while its lines and colour made it stand out in a sea of Villiers-powered lightweights.

The machine continued in this form for a year, but for 1950 was modified a little and joined by a host of other versions including

The 1964 D7 was little altered; the model would run on for two more years.

which allowed the lead to sweep back, up and round to the plug. Elsewhere the centre stand lost its clip and gained a return spring, the front forks were given gaiters and the exhaust pipe was run above the footrest instead of below it.

Options extended the range to eight models by combining the existing specification with plunger rear suspension, Lucas electrics or a competition build in any permutation. The plungers were a simple adaptation of the rigid Bantam frame with a typical BSA design of load and return springs concealed by covers. With it came a rear mudguard with deep valance all the way round and a rear hub with stronger spindle.

The Lucas electrics gave the machine coil ignition with a special alternator and its own support casting in place of the usual items. In addition to these obvious changes, the crankshaft also differed as the left mainshaft was much shorter and the flywheel rim thicker and heavier to maintain the inertia despite the lighter rotor.

some exports finished in black. The changes did not amount to much and the most obvious was to the Wipac generator. This took on a smoother shape, with a much larger cover over the points and a lead exit

The D7 Silver was an economy machine built for 1966 in its final year for that model series. It was finished with minimal chrome plating.

The Lucas system had a battery and rectifier, with the ignition coil mounted on a frame bracket under the tank. It was controlled by a combination ignition/lighting switch set in the headlamp shell, along with an ammeter.

The competition models, like the road ones, could have the rigid or plunger frame and Wipac or Lucas electrics, although rigid and Wipac was normal. The other changes were minor with the silencer tilted up, saddle raised, footrests modified and rear tyre increased in section. A decompressor appeared in the front of the cylinder head, using a sparking plug thread, and there were taper roller bearings in the front hub and a folding kickstart pedal. Blade mudguards were fitted and the gearing lowered by a larger rear sprocket which gave an unexpected bonus. The resulting higher engine speed helped to avoid condensation in the crankcase, which could ruin the main bearings of the road models with their high top gear.

There were no changes for 1951, but for 1952 the frame headstock gusset was strengthened and the light switch of the Wipac models moved to the headlight shell. For 1953 the big end was given longer rollers so the flywheels had to be recessed. On the outside, the front mudguard became unsprung and was without a valance, while pillion rest lugs were added to the frame and chrome strips to decorate the tank top seams. The standard colour remained mist green but with an option in black, while the wheel rims were chrome plated in either case. The saddle remained the usual seat, but a dualseat appeared as an option and this was to remain so for all rigid and plunger road Bantams.

At the end of the year the Lucas electrics option was dropped, so four D1 models went forward for 1954 as rigid or plunger, road or competition machines with Wipac direct lighting. They were joined by two more with battery lights, and rigid or plunger frames to replace the Lucas-equipped road models, and all had changes.

All engines had a new head and barrel with deeper fins, and the road models also changed to a tubular silencer and gained a headlamp cowl. The competition models kept to the flat silencer but were fitted with heavier front forks and a slightly larger front brake.

The D1 Bantams were joined by four 148 cc D3 models which were similar but had the bore enlarged to 57 mm to give the extra capacity. There were two road models which had plunger rear suspension and kept the option of direct or battery lighting. The competition ones only had the option of rigid or plunger frames, but all the D3 models mirrored the equivalent D1 machines except that *all* had the heavier front fork, not just the competition versions.

The D1 and D3 competition models with plunger frames were dropped at the end of the year, but the others ran on for 1955. Then for 1956, all but the plunger frame D1 with direct or battery lighting were dropped. These two remaining machines were joined by two new D3 types with the same electrical variation. They kept the same engine as before but installed this in a frame with pivoted fork rear suspension, a dualseat as standard and a long, tapered silencer. A saddle was offered as an option and the D3 was finished in grey, as was usual, with both D1 and D3 available in black or maroon as well.

There were no changes for 1957, but for 1958 the D3 was replaced by the 172 cc D5. The extra capacity came from boring the engine out to 61.5 mm, and for this there

During 1966 the D10 range took over with the points moved to the right and a better alternator but the same 172 cc capacity. This was the economy Silver model which was the cheapest listed.

was a new barrel with flange-mounted carburettor. Inside there was a caged roller big end and a rearrangement of the oil seals so that all the main bearings were lubricated by the gearbox oil via various catchments, holes and drains. The D5 cycle side was similar to the D3 with pivoted rear fork, but the brake shoes were wider and the tyres altered to 3.00x18 in. The fuel tank was deeper and the finish maroon, with no options for both direct and battery lighting versions.

The D5 was only an interim step, for it was replaced by the D7 for 1959 with this listed as the Super in either electrical form. The engine gained an extra cover on the left to enclose both the magneto and clutch adjuster, but was otherwise as for the D5. The frame was new with hydraulically damped front forks with a nacelle for the headlamp, and the machine had the larger brakes but in new, cast-iron hubs. Mudguards and handlebars were also new, while the side panels for toolbox and battery were blended into a centre panel.

The D1 had continued as it was and both it and the D7 remained unchanged until 1962, when the larger engines were given a needle roller small end. At the end of 1963 the D1 was finally dropped, to the dismay of many owners, for BSA planned to replace it with the Beagle. The D7 was joined by a de luxe version for 1964 when it was given a revised silencer and magnetic speedometer head.

For 1966 the models became the D7 de luxe, with minor changes to the tank and centre panels, and the D7 Silver, an econ-

The D10 Supreme offered a better finish with more chrome plating than the Silver but was still much as the D5 of some years back.

omy job with silver sheen finish. Both were replaced in July that year by the D10 range which represented a significant change for the Bantam engine. The most obvious was a small cover on the chaincase that concealed the contact points which were separated from the generator. This remained where it was but changed to a six-pole alternator which greatly improved the electrical side. Some early D10 models fitted Amal Monobloc carburettors, but most came with the later Amal Concentric. In either case the size was increased and this plus a raised compression ratio gave the engine more power, so the clutch had an extra plate fitted to deal with it.

The D10 Silver and Supreme models effectively replaced the D7 ones and retained the three-speed gearbox. The other two models had a new four-speed box which was fitted in the same space although gears, change mechanism and crankcase were all new. In addition, the clutch bush lost its flange, to become plain, but gained a thrust washer. The first new model was the D10 Sports which had a separate headlamp shell, waist-level exhaust system, dualseat with hump, flyscreen and full-width hubs. The second was the D10 Bushman built for trail use with suitable tyres on 19 in. rims, upswept exhaust, revised gearing, separate headlamp and a crankcase shield.

These D10 models did not last long and were replaced by the D14 series for 1968, all of which had the four-speed gearbox and a larger diameter exhaust pipe. Of the three models the D14/4 replaced the Supreme, the D14/4S the Sports and the D14/4B the Bushman. The last two had heavier duty front forks with gaiters and a front brake backplate with a torque arm.

The final chapter in the Bantam saga began for 1969 with the appearance of the D175 road and Bushman models. Despite the problems the firm had begun to experience, these had much revised engines with new crankcase castings and cylinder head with central sparking plug. Inside, there was a stiffer crankshaft, while externally it was back to offset hubs.

In this final form the Bantam entered the 1970s, but only the standard model was

The D10 Sportsman had a much-needed four-speed gearbox along with a host of fitments to suit the image it was intended to give—rather distant from that of the first D1.

The final D10 model of 1966 was the off-road Bushman combining the four-speed engine with suitable cycle parts for the trail market.

listed for 1971. It was almost ignored at the firm's last major model launch and soon faded from the lists in March. Thus, no longer did BSA have a commuter model in its range, or one for novices or messengers.

At least 200,000 Bantams were built during the model's twenty-three-year life span, and many still survive. A large number of these would seem to have had an engine change at some time, so matching engine and frame numbers are now uncommon. Since all engines will fit all frames the mechanical change is easy to make, but the electrics can be more awkward to sort out. So this is an essential point to check when buying.

Many Bantams were built for road racing, especially in the 1960s and 1970s, so don't be surprised to find evidence of this. Some changes will not be compatible with road

For 1968 the D14 replaced the D10 but kept the 172 cc and four speeds so was built in Supreme, as here, Sportsman and Bushman versions.

use, but most can be lived with. Just make sure you know what is there.

Prospects

Bantams never rate more than three stars because, no matter how good, they are still a small two-stroke and will not command the interest that the larger four-strokes get. Generally, old is better than new, and the rarer models are more valuable than the more common ones.

Thus the early D1, any competition model, D5 and Bushman D10 or D14 command three stars. Then there are two stars for many run-of-the mill models, with only one star for the readily available. Late D1 and

The final Bantam appeared for 1969 as the 175 Bantam or D175 and had a number of engine changes which included the central sparking plug.

most D7 machines fall into this category, but with all Bantams the buyer must ask whether the engine and frame match. If they do, then a nice example could gain half a star at least; if they don't match, then it loses the same as long as the two halves are of a type.

There are variants of this, however; a plunger D1 with D3 engine is fairly acceptable, as is the reverse, while a plunger frame with any 172 cc engine is much less so. Equally, a Bushman with a D7 engine is not a good build, for a better engine would be quite easy to find.

Frames and cycle parts can also become mixed, and a further trap for the unwary may be parts from the Triumph Tiger Cub. This machine shared fork legs and hubs with the D7 for some years, and in its final form used many Bantam parts. This is not necessarily a problem as long as you know about it.

With the restrictions that exist in the United Kingdom to keep novice riders to a maximum of 125 cc, there can be a temptation to modify a Bantam to its D1 size. This can be done with a D3 engine but not the others due to variations in the cylinder stud centres. Even with the early D1 and D3 there were differences, so care is needed if this course is followed. To alter a 172 cc engine would involve much work and cost, so it is not worth considering. Better to buy an old Honda 50, pass your test and then sell it again, the expense will be much less.

The Bantam is an excellent way of owning a BSA at a reasonable cost, and any restoration needed should be quite easy to carry out. The models and most running spares are readily available and there is plenty of information available for keeping them on the road.

The final model was also available as the D175B Bushman model, which continued in the same theme as the others before it with trail tyres, undershield and more ground clearance.

Chapter 2

Flyweights and scooters

★	Winged Wheel	1953–55
★★★	Beeza	1955
★	Dandy	1957–62
★	Beagle	1964–65
★	Sunbeam B1	1960–65
★★	Sunbeam B2	1959–64
★★	Sunbeam B2S	1959–64
	Easy Rider	1979–85
	Beaver	1979–81
	Brigand	1979–81
	Boxer	1979–80
	GT50	1980–83
	Tracker	1979–87
	Junior	1979–87

BSA made limited attempts to enter the bottom end of the market with cyclemotor, scooterette, moped and scooter, but none of these worked out well. It seemed that its forte was good, solid, reliable motorcycles and while the firm kept to this it did well; diversions seldom seemed to pay off.

Flyweights

Included in the flyweights class is the Winged Wheel, which was BSA's unit for the cyclemotor market. The firm was really some years too late when it launched the Winged Wheel in May 1953, for the type was essentially an immediate postwar form of transport. As a means of taking the hard work out of riding a bicycle, bolting a small engine in place went back to the origins of motorcycling.

During the late 1940s there were many shortages and few new vehicles in most countries, so the cyclemotor represented the cheapest way to have motorised transport. It was taken up with enthusiasm by cyclists tired of pedalling, but its shortcomings were soon apparent and in a few years the moped replaced it. Since BSA already made bicycles, it should have reacted faster, but at the time motorcycles would have been more profitable and the company had material shortages to contend with as well.

Once the firm decided to go ahead with the cyclemotor, it sought to produce a better vehicle than most, so the common friction drive from serrated roller to tyre idea was not used. Instead, it chose to offer a proper transmission including a clutch, with the whole unit built into a cycle rear wheel. This substituted for the original, and a fuel tank, formed as a carrier, was added above the rear mudguard.

The wheel was powered by a 34.6 cc two-stroke engine which had its cast-iron cylinder horizontal on the left below the chain stay. The cooling fins ran along both barrel and separate alloy head while the built-up crankshaft had full flywheels. The Wipac flywheel magneto went on the left end of the crankshaft and the mixture was supplied by a small down-draught Amal. The exhaust and silencer box was tucked neatly below the crankcase, with a short tailpipe to the rear.

The right end of the crankshaft carried a pinion which meshed with a gear cut in the clutch drum. The clutch itself had three driven plates with cork inserts and was clamped up by ten small springs. The shaft it ran on, and to which its centre was splined, carried a further pinion on its inboard end, with this meshed with a further gear. This was positioned on the rear wheel spindle axis and riveted to a 9½ in. drum, which enclosed the transmission and provided the rear brake surface. The rim was spoked to this drum inside which were the two shoes, each with its own pivot, but operated by a single cam.

The wheel was easily fitted to most standard bicycles and the extra controls were simply throttle and clutch, for the rear brake connected to the usual lever. The carburettor had a choke, but this was linked to the throttle slide to come into operation when the throttle lever was moved past the full-open position. A stop prevented this in normal riding with a trigger to release it.

The complete Wheel sold for £25 and offered 20 mph cruising, fine for 1953 traffic. By 1955 a complete machine was also offered by the BSA group, with the choice of crossbar or drop frames. In either case, light Webb blade girder forks were fitted but by then the market was beginning to turn to the moped, as exemplified by the NSU Quickly.

The day of the cyclemotor was effectively over and BSA sensibly withdrew the Wheel and used its resources for other machines.

These innovations were first seen by the public at Earls Court late in 1955 when the firm exhibited a scooter and scooterette.

The first was called the Beeza, or Beezer, and had a 198 cc side-valve engine at a time when scooter buyers were more used to two-strokes of 150 cc. The design had engine, transmission and rear wheel assembled as one unit which was pivoted from the frame to provide the rear suspension.

The driveline and crankshaft ran along on the right, so the all-alloy engine was horizontal with the cylinder pointing to the left. The valves went above it at an angle and were opened by bellcrank cam followers with adjusters built in. The camshaft had the points with their automatic advance at its front end and was driven by a train of gears

The BSA Winged Wheel bicycle was available as a ladies or gents model fitted with the light girder forks in either case.

Dandy scooterette with inaccessible contact points and awkward pre-selector gearchange made little impact when the NSU Quickly was cheap, available and worked much better.

from the front of the engine where the alternator was fitted.

Inside went a forged crankshaft with split connecting rod and plain bearings. It ran in ball and plain mains and also drove a stock

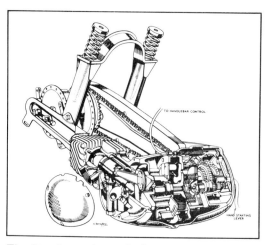

The Dandy engine as built up to form the rear suspension fork with a pressing bolted to the cylinder head. All this had to come apart to set the points gap.

BSA gear oil pump for the dry-sump lubrication system. The mixture was supplied by an Amal carburettor tucked in behind the cylinder, and the exhaust pipe ran round to a silencer on the left.

A single-plate clutch went on the rear of the crankshaft and its flywheel was gearcut to mesh with a Lucas electric starter. The drive ran back from the clutch to an all-indirect four-speed gearbox, with the output shaft outboard and higher than the input. The gears were selected by a positive stop mechanism which was controlled by two pedals, with one each for up and down changes.

The gearbox drove back with a short shaft to a pair of spiral bevel gears driving the rear hub. All the mechanics were enclosed in a series of alloy castings to form one unit, and its pivot point was above the gearbox. Movement was controlled by a single spring and damper unit on the right with this anchored to the subframe.

The mainframe was a single tube that was welded to the headstock and ran down and then back before changing to twin D-section tubes formed into a rectangle. Plates carried the main pivot point, with the subframe bolted in place and braced for the spring unit loads. There was a bolted-on support for the body at the front and an oil tank on the left, while the petrol tank went above the rear wheel.

Front suspension was by leading links controlled by a spring on each side wound to be loaded torsionally, with the link movement restricted by rubber stops. The wheels were interchangeable with 12 in. pressed steel rims and the hubs had drum brakes. A typical scooter body went over all the mechanics but had a separate front mudguard and deep tunnel behind the apron.

The Beeza was an interesting project but by 1956 the Italian scooters dominated the market, while the top end was the preserve of larger, more expensive, German products. The BSA fell between them, for its performance was not up to that of the German machines while its looks were too heavy to compare with the Italians. Finally, BSA decided the Beeza was too costly to make, so the machine never did go into production.

The Beagle shared many engine design points with the Ariel Pixie but lacked its style. Having a 75 cc ohv engine was no great asset, although economical in use.

The scooterette, another new design, was the 70 cc Dandy, much lighter but just as unusual as the Beeza in its own way. The frame was typical moped with steel pressings welded together but with the centre area dropped to make it a step-through. At the front were pressed steel forks with leading links controlled by undamped compression springs, while the rear of the frame had a carrier fitted to it. Just ahead of this went the saddle with the fuel tank under it but on top of the frame. Large legshields ran down and back under the rider's feet to give plenty of protection, and the rear mudguard was well valanced over its front quarter.

The engine, transmission and rear pivoted fork were formed as one unit but not in the same manner as the Beeza's. The engine was a two-stroke with the head and barrel forming part of the right fork leg, with an extension bolted to the head studs to reach back to the wheel spindle. The cylinder was thus horizontal, and the crankcase ran across the machine ahead of the rear wheel. In it went an overhung crankshaft, and outboard of

A Beagle in action late in 1963 when its large wheels helped to give it a good ride on poor road surfaces, assisted by the leading link front forks.

the end cover was the small carburettor under its own outer cover.

The crankshaft extended to the left with first the flywheel magneto and then the clutch. This placed the points in the middle of the engine where access to them meant a major dismantling job. The clutch output shaft carried a gear at its end, and this meshed with one on the input shaft of the two-speed gearbox. Gear selection took place on the output shaft behind it, from which a chain drove the rear wheel. The gearbox thus lay on the left side of the machine and a further fork leg was bolted to it.

Gear engagement was by a pre-selector device operated by a lever mounted on the handlebars and an arrangement of springs controlling the selector fork. The lever was first set to the desired gear but this was not engaged until the clutch was withdrawn, which was fine in theory but less so in practice. The springs had to work against each other which is never good design, and the whole arrangement was overly complex compared to the common twistgrip change used by many mopeds and scooters.

Although the Dandy was shown to the public late in 1955, it was a year before production got under way for 1957. The next year it had some revisions to the gear change, which had not proved successful, and the stand and rear brake. From then on it continued with only colour variations until 1962 when it was dropped, rather to the relief of the trade.

Not a firm to give up, BSA had one more go at the flyweight market in an exercise that also involved the Ariel company, which was part of the BSA empire. The result was the BSA Beagle and Ariel Pixie which shared common engine component parts, although their capacities were 75 cc and 50 cc respectively. The appearance of the two machines differed a good deal as did most of their cycle specification.

The engine was a simple ohv four-stroke with inclined cylinder and four-speed gearbox in unit. It reduced to a minimum of parts, with the main crankcase split on the engine centre line but carrying the whole gearbox in the right side. A single cover then enclosed both box internals and timing gear,

with an outer cover over the change mechanism.

The iron barrel spigoted into the case with an alloy head held on the same four long studs. The rocker boxes were integral and sealed by lids while the valves were opened by a single, gear-driven camshaft. A single-plunger oil pump dealt with the wet-sump lubrication, while a flywheel magneto on the left provided ignition. The crankshaft was pressed up with plain big end and ran in ball races.

The clutch and gearbox were conventional in most respects, with the gears selected by a quadrant face cam much as in the BSA unit singles. The one odd feature lay in the primary drive which was by gears, with the engine pinion meshed with gear teeth cut onto the clutch friction plates, so no drum was needed.

This neat engine unit was hung from a spine frame built up from pressings and fitted with pivoted fork rear suspension. At the front were short leading link forks while both wheels had well-valanced mudguards and 19 in. rims spoked to hubs with small drum brakes. There was a single seat and small tank, so the machine lines were light motorcycle and none too modern compared with the Pixie which was far more stylish.

The Beagle was announced late in 1962 but it was another year before models began to reach the shops. By then, time was running out, as it had to sell against the Honda step-through models and lacked their weather protection. The machine stayed in the range for 1965 but during that year was quietly dropped.

Prospects

Only the Beeza rates more than one star among the flyweights, and that is only because it never went into production. The Wheel, Dandy and Beagle are collectible models to few people so sit low down in the pecking order.

There are groups of enthusiasts for such basic transport, but their numbers are small and, aside from them, there is little demand or interest in these models.

Scooters

After the Beeza, BSA made one more attempt on the scooter market and produced a range in conjunction with Triumph. It came too late, however; by the time the press launch was held late in 1958 the existence of the machines was well known. Furthermore, BSA again failed to grasp the needs of the scooter market and to realize what had to be done to break the hold the Italian models had on it.

There were three models in the range that was launched under the Sunbeam label, and these were duplicated as Triumphs by changing colour and badges. There were two capacities with the smaller 172 cc two-stroke based on the Bantam, and the other a 249 cc ohv twin offered with kick or electric starting. The machines were listed as the B1, B2 and B2S respectively.

The models shared mechanical and body-work parts from the clutch onward despite the differences in the engine types. The smaller copied the Bantam in design but not parts as few were common, but remained a basic two-stroke with a fan attached to the flywheel magneto on the right to assist the cooling under a top-half cowling.

The left mainshaft was extended to reach the clutch and this then drove back to a four-speed gearbox. Again, the internals were derived from the BSA unit singles, and the positive stop mechanism was linked to twin pedals with one each for up or down changes. The final drive was by a duplex chain running on fixed centres with a slipper tensioner, and this was fully enclosed in an alloy case acting as the rear suspension pivoted arm.

The twin-cylinder engine had one main alloy casting to form the block, crankcase and gearbox, with a forged crankshaft and gear-driven camshaft. The valves sat inline

The Beezer scooter had somewhat heavy lines concealing a 198 cc side-valve engine built in unit with the four-speed gearbox and final drive. The Beezer was never to reach production.

BSA/Sunbeam scooter following a Triumph Tigress during an ACU (Auto-Cycle Union) observed run to publicize the two marques. Both used the same parts with just badges and colour to distinguish them.

in the alloy head but with the outer exhaust valves splayed and the rockers arranged to suit. A single-plunger pump kept the wet-sump lubrication in order, ignition was by coil and the alternator on the right had both a cooling fan and starter gear ring.

The rest of the twin was as for the single and both used the same tubular frame. This had the headstock bolted to the two down-tubes, but was otherwise much as other scooter frames. The front forks were single sided, with a left leg housing both spring and damper units. A single unit controlled the rear end, and both 10 in. pressed steel wheels ran on stub axles and had hubs with 5 in. drum brakes.

The body was conventional scooter and there was little to distinguish one model from another except the badges. Minor tell-tales were the silencers, with the single's under the engine with the tailpipe on the right, while the twin's was in the tail of the body with a rear exit. Another difference was the battery boxes which went on the rear of the apron, with one for the kickstart model and two where electric starting was provided. A good range of accessories were listed for all models, for these were always an important part of a scooter sale. Often a dealer would profit as much from accessories as from the machine itself.

The range was launched with style and considerable expense but failed to strike a note with the public. The smaller model was heavy and lacked the verve of the Italians, while the larger failed to worry the big-capacity German models.

The twin went on the market early in 1959 with the single following later, but sales were disappointing. There were some colour changes but little else, and the twins were withdrawn in 1964 and the single the next year.

Prospects

Two stars for the scooter twins and one for the single although few people ride, collect or restore old scooters. There is a club for them, albeit none too large, but otherwise there is little interest either for riding or investment.

If scooters are your thing, then the twin with electric start and plenty of accessories will be the one to go for. The single is rare, which could be taken as an asset to a collector or a benefit to others.

Modern flyweights

After the collapse of the BSA group in the early 1970s few expected to see the name on a motorcycle again. The group became part of the Norton-Villiers-Triumph trio (NVT)

The BSA/Sunbeam scooter at Lands End on the last day of the run, which failed to convince enough people that they should buy either make or size.

which continued to lurch through the decade in a series of commercial convolutions. Finally, in 1979, the BSA came back but with little that was exciting.

Most of the models were of 50 cc, and at the bottom came two versions of the Easy Rider moped which first had been seen with the NVT label. BSA used an Italian Morini engine with single speed for the ER1 and automatic two-speed for the ER2, which improved performance by giving better acceleration. The two-stroke engine had the cylinder horizontal so it tucked under the single tube of the frame. This went up and down along the machine and formed the fuel tank at the front while supporting saddle, carrier and units for the suspension at the rear.

The other two machines launched early in 1979 were the Beaver for road use and the Brigand as a trail bike. Both had the same 50

BSA Beaver restricted moped of 1979 with its imported engine. The monoshock rear suspension worked well enough at the speeds the machine could reach.

Brigand off-road moped with the Beaver engine and frame, but raised matt black exhaust system, braced bars, 19 in. front wheel and trail tyres to help it along.

cc two-stroke engine with four-speed gearbox housed in a duplex cradle frame with monoshock rear suspension. The specification was fairly basic with wire spoke wheels and drum brakes, but did include turn signals. The Beaver had road mudguards and a low-level exhaust system, while the Brigand was decked out with raised guards and exhaust with the latter finished in matt black.

Both models had a restricted power output to conform to the UK moped requirements of the time, but were joined later that year by the derestricted Boxer. This was much as the Beaver but with more power and a black and gold finish set off by stainless steel mudguards.

Further up the range there were two trail machines listed under the name Tracker with 125 or 175 cc engines. Both were Yamaha units with six-speed gearboxes installed in frames with monoshock rear and telescopic fork front suspension. Fixtures and fittings were to suit off-road use, but neither model was too popular.

To complete its list, BSA offered the Junior which used a kickstart version of the Easy Rider single-speed engine in miniature

The Boxer was the de-restricted version of the Beaver and thus similar in most respects but with more speed and acceleration.

motocross cycle parts. It was aimed at the child market and its simple chassis kept the monoshock rear, while the red or blue finish for the one-piece tank cover, seat base and side panels set it off well.

These models kept the BSA name alive into the new decade with the Boxer being renamed the GT50 for 1980. Late that year the ER2 was dropped, and during 1981 the remaining moped was replaced by revised models with a reed valve engine and, for one, a kickstart. The Beaver and Brigand were dropped that year but the GT50, Trackers, Junior and new Easy Riders ran on. Later came variants for the military in 125 and 175 cc capacities, plus one of 250 cc and also models for trail parks. These were the 125 and 175 cc BTX models based on the Tracker but minus lights and other easily damaged road equipment.

The Junior was joined by a JTX version still aimed at the same age group but offering a more sophisticated off-road specification. This included hydraulically damped suspension, raised exhaust and cast-alloy wheels, the last perhaps an odd choice.

All in all, it was a period when a small company concentrated on survival and did just that by adapting to the needs with the materials that came to hand. Would that the management of two or three decades earlier had shown as much enterprise.

Prospects

Not a star in sight for modern flyweights; who wants to know about mopeds, foreign-engined models or miniature motorcycles? If you find one and it is virtually given away and you have a use or a passing interest, then please, take it into your stable. Do not expect to be able to sell it again, however, much less see it as any form of investment.

The 125 Tracker used a Yamaha engine and gearbox unit in a frame with monoshock rear suspension and trail equipment. Also available with a 175 engine.

The GT50 was the Boxer with a new name for 1980, here seen waiting its turn in the workshop.

As a machine they worked quite well but were never to challenge the major firms.

Chapter 3

B group and Gold Stars

★★★	B31, rigid	1945–54
★★★	B31, plunger	1949–55
★★★	B31, swing arm	1954–59
★★★★	B32, rigid	1946–55
★★★★	B32, plunger	1949–53
★★★★	B32, swing arm	1954–57
★★★	B33, rigid	1947–54
★★★	B33, plunger	1949–55
★★★	B33, swing arm	1954–60
★★★★	B34, rigid	1947–55
★★★★	B34, plunger	1949–53
★★★★	B34, swing arm	1954–57
★★★★	B31/B33 alloy engine option	1950
★★★★	B32 scrambles special	1949
★★★★	B32 scrambles special plunger	1949
★★★★	B32/B34 plus Gold Star engine	1950–51
★★★★	B32/B34 alloy engine option	1950–53
★★★★	B32/B34 alloy engine standard	1954–57
Gold Star		
★★★★★	B32/B34 ZB, plunger	1949–52
★★★★★	B32/B34 BB	1953–55
★★★★★	B32/B34 CB	1954–55
★★★★★	B32 DB	1955–57
★★★★★	B32 DB	1959–62
★★★★★	B34 DB	1955–57
★★★★★	B34 DBD	1956–63
★★★★★	Tourer	1949–56
★★★★★	Trials	1950–55
★★★★★	ISDT	1953–54
★★★★★	Scrambles	1950–63
★★★★★	Racing	1950–57
★★★★★	Clubman	1950–63

All the postwar B range machines, whether prosaic road or glamourous Clubmans, had their roots in the prewar models introduced for 1937. This line was designed by Val Page, and for it he drew on his experience of similar machines at Ariel and Triumph. The result was a series of simple ohv engines that were to prove both reliable and strong. At the same time he revised the gearbox and frame so he could produce a strong range with the minimum of basic items.

There were effectively two ranges, one the B models of 250 and 350 cc intended for solo work only, and the other the M range of 350, 500 or 600 cc and more heavily built. The latter were intended for solo or sidecar use, and both ranges included engines with side or overhead valves, three- or four-speed gearboxes and hand or foot change. All had rigid frames, girder forks and that essential BSA rugged construction.

The prewar range prospered and in time was modified to include the lightweight C models dealt with in the next chapter. It also produced two models that had a significant effect on the postwar range. The first to appear was the Gold Star, listed prosaically as the M24 and offered in road, competition and track forms, while the second was the B29.

The Gold Star was based on the sporting Empire Star and took its name from the award given to all who lapped the bumpy Brooklands outer circuit at over 100 mph during a race. One such was won by Wal Handley in June 1937 riding a tuned Empire Star running on alcohol fuel. With Handley's skill and experience he won his race and lapped at over 107 mph, so the name of the new 1938 machine was inevitable.

The M24 was of 496 cc with an all-alloy bench-tested engine, TT Amal carburettor, Electron alloy gearbox shell and lighter gauge frame tubes without any sidecar lugs. It had a crankcase shield and a toolbox set in the top of the petrol tank which was chrome plated with matt silver panels. The competition version was modified for trials use with narrow mudguards, competition tyres and upswept exhaust, while the track version was set up to run on alcohol fuel and for Brooklands. It is unlikely that any of the latter were ever made.

The Gold Star had a lukewarm reception, for its show debut was overshadowed by the new Triumph Speed Twin. It failed to appeal to the sporting rider who looked for a company with a racing background, while the traditional BSA owner tended to prefer the Empire Star. The engine was also noisy and the gear change and handling were nothing to write home about.

The machine was modified a little for 1939 with a change to a separate toolbox and tank

The first new postwar model was the 348 cc B31, which gave good performance and in time was to lead to much more sporting models as well as the larger B33.

A B31 during the first year with the pivoted-fork frame which was 1954. The dualseat was still an extra. The engine and gearbox was as before and the headlamp cowl continued.

top instrument panel. It meant that the machine had the same sports lines as others in the range and this limited its appeal to the buying public. It was not retained in the abortive 1940 range, which was quickly cut short by the outbreak of World War II, and it was nine years before the name appeared again.

The B29 did not appear until 1940 when it, and the 348 cc C12, replaced the whole of the existing B range. It was a 348 cc ohv model that combined the traditional BSA solo weight cycle parts with the M range bottom half with stiffer crankcase. It had hairpin valve springs but was otherwise of typical BSA construction in all areas, even though only a few were made.

During the war the model was developed into the WB30, covered more fully in chapter nine, and after it as the B31. This dispensed with the hairpin springs but established a whole line of good, solid, no-nonsense models plus sporting derivatives.

Road B models

The road B models were the B31 and B33 introduced just after the war and from which the competition and Gold Star machines were derived. They developed along with the times to the end of the 1950s, but always remained middleweight tourers.

The B31 was announced in August 1945 and had a simple, all-iron, ohv engine driving a four-speed gearbox with footchange, all installed in a rigid, open-diamond frame equipped with telescopic front forks. The 348 cc engine followed traditional lines with a built-up crankshaft with roller big end turning in ball and roller mains. The crankcase was split on its vertical centre line with the barrel spigoted into it and the head to the barrel. The only unusual feature was the design of the four hold-down bolts which were restrained by inserts in the crankcase and screwed into the underside of the head to hold both it and the barrel.

The rocker box was cast integral with the head and had an access cover over each valve and fixed hollow spindles for the rockers. Each was lubricated by a supply pipe connected to the main return line, and the oil drained into the valve wells and then to the crankcase via internal drillings and an external pipe.

The rockers were moved by pushrods which ran up from the crankcase in a tower held up at the top by a large gland nut. The cams sat side by side in the timing chest on the right with tappets to move the pushrods and gears to drive them. The gear train ran on to a rear-mounted mag-dyno and was supported by a bushed plate and enclosed by a single outer cover.

The duplex gear oil pump for the dry-sump lubrication system went into the base of the right crankcase where it was driven by a skew gear on the crankshaft. Its position required the casting to swell out to enclose it, a feature that proved awkward when the engine was mounted in a cradle frame. To clear it the frame tube was kinked; this became a common BSA identification point.

The rest of the B31 was just as traditional with a single-strand primary chain driving a multi-plate clutch. A pressed steel chaincase enclosed the transmission, and its multiple small screws helped keep the oil inside it better than many others. The clutch drove a typical English four-speed gearbox with gear change and kickstart pedals on the right, and this drove the rear wheel with an exposed chain.

Engine and gearbox went into a built-up rigid frame with the front half comprising top, down and seat tubes. The chain and seat stays formed the rear part which bolted in place with plates to hold the gearbox. At the front were the excellent BSA telescopic forks with hydraulic damping and a friction steering damper.

Both wheels had 19 in. rims spoked to offset hubs with 7 in. brakes, and were quick and easy to remove. At the front the spindle was clamped in one fork leg and screwed, with a left-hand thread, into the other. For the rear, the first 1945 design was soon

Restored 1955 B31 with pivoted-fork frame. The parts list shows a valanced front mudguard only for the B33 while the petrol pipe will vapour lock if left with that coil.

replaced by a quickly detachable design whose format is still much used. It comprised a spline drive between sprocket drum and hub, distance piece between hub bearing and frame, with a spindle through the lot to hold it all in place.

The remainder of the details consisted of an Amal carburettor, low-level exhaust system on the right, saddle, battery on left, oil tank on right, toolbox between the chain stays and petrol tank. The latter housed the speedometer in its top with the drive from the gearbox. There were centre and front stands but no prop, which was a pity since BSA never did seem to provide a decent centre stand that could be used without strain.

The B31 provided just what was needed at the time, with enough speed for the narrow, twisty roads of the period, comfort, good handling and reliability. There was nothing exceptional about it, but in 1946 any transport was good news and most alternatives were ex-army models which were a good deal less inspiring.

During 1946 the rear hub design was revised to the famous crinkle hub, allowing the use of straight spokes. It remained a favourite for a decade or more and continued to offer the quickly detachable facility. There were few other changes, however; in those days the number of machines built meant far more than innovation.

For 1947 BSA responded to public demand by producing a larger model in the form of the 499 cc B33. This had an increased bore and heavier flywheels but was otherwise a replica of the B31 with a fatter rear tyre and raised gearing on the cycle side. During the year it gained a silver strip down the centre of each mudguard, but one suspects this was just to aid the factory and their dealers when counting stock. Both machines were finished in black with the tank chrome plated with matt silver panels, so they were hard to tell apart.

The speedometer was moved from the tank to the top of the forks for both models for 1948 along with other minor changes, but there were also options for the finish. The B31 could have its tank panels and wheel rim centres in Brunswick green, while the B33 optional colour was Devon red. Both proved popular and from then on the options were seen as much as the standard matt silver.

There were further changes for 1949 with the most obvious the option of plunger rear suspension. This was of a typical BSA form with bump and rebound springs concealed by metal covers and no damping other than the friction of the assembly. At the same time the transmission was rationalised, so one gearbox suited several ranges including the B range, and the dynamo was improved.

For 1950 only there was an alloy engine option listed for the road B models, although it seems unlikely that any were ever supplied. Otherwise, the two machines continued with their uneventful lives, taking owners to work and play with little excitement. A dualseat option appeared for 1952, and for 1953 there was a boxed-in rear number plate, headlamp cowl, underslung pilot lamp and an 8 in. front brake for the B33. That model was also fitted with a valanced front mudguard which carried its number plates on each side.

During this period changes had more to do with the finish because of a world shortage of nickel. Thus, during 1952, the tanks were simply painted green or red for the two models, with gold linings and wheel rims to match. By 1953 this situation had improved and the finish became maroon for all painted parts, with chrome-plated tank side panels for all, plus an option in black.

A new frame with pivoted fork rear suspension appeared for 1954, but both rigid

This is the 1957 B33 with rear chaincase to enclose the chain and full-width alloy hubs as well as the cast-alloy primary chaincase.

and plunger models continued alongside as it was destined for export only at first. All were still finished in maroon for painted parts, but the 1953 option of all-black was no longer listed.

The pivoted fork frame had first been seen on the Gold Star models and was of all-welded construction with a single top tube braced by a smaller one beneath it. The rest of the main loop was duplex with the kink in the right one to clear the oil pump. Loops to the rear supported the tops of the spring units, the seat and the mudguard with small loops for the pillion rests. The rear fork was tubular and controlled by Girling units inclined forward a little, and a centre stand was fitted to the mainframe.

The engines fitted to the new frame were as before but the gears went into a new shell and there were new engine plates at front and rear. The forks stayed as before as did the wheels, but most of the rest had to be altered to suit the new design. The petrol tank mounting was simplified so that a single bolt, with an array of steel and rubber washers, held it down by screwing into a lug on the top frame tube. Rubber pads and buffers held the tank firm and it was thus less stressed and easier to remove.

The oil tank also changed and became slimmer and tucked into the right frame loop, with a toolbox of the same shape on the left to match it. The battery sat on a platform between them and a dualseat was fitted as standard. A polished alloy primary chaincase replaced the pressed steel type, and the tank badges became round plastic with the piled arms insignia moulded in.

The rigid models were dropped at the end of the year, but the plunger models continued and the pivoted fork frame became a home market option. With this frame the engines were fitted with the new Amal Monobloc carburettor, but the plunger models kept to the older type. All machines gained a steering lock in the top fork crown and lost the underslung pilot lamp, while the engine shock absorber cam altered to a two-lobe form.

For 1956, only the pivoted fork frame models were kept in the range, and they retained their maroon finish but with the

black option listed once more. The only change was to the hubs which became full-width, light alloy, with 7 in. brakes in both wheels. They were from the Ariel range, this company being part of the BSA group, and had wide shoes with the adjuster built into their fulcrum. The rear brake was cable operated from a cross-shaft that ran through the centre of the rear fork pivot, with a lever on one side and the brake pedal on the other.

The new hub retained the quick-detachable facility, and this allowed BSA to offer an optional full chaincase. This was in three parts and helped to keep the machine clean and tidy, so was a worthwhile addition to have.

There were no changes to the B31 and B33 for 1957, but the next year the two models moved to their final form. The major change

The B33 in its USA form for 1957 with high rise bars and a handrail running around the dualseat but otherwise much as the standard model.

Near the end of its time, a 1959 B33 with the composite full-width hubs but really the same engine as first seen in 1947 and much the same gearbox.

to the engine was the adoption of an alternator and coil ignition. The first went on the left end of the crankshaft and required a change to the primary chaincase to accommodate it. The second brought in a points housing which went in the old mag-dyno position, with the same gear drive but with auto advance incorporated.

These changes meant alterations to the wiring and switches plus the movement of the shock absorber into the clutch centre. The switches were mounted in a nacelle which replaced the cowl of 1953 and carried the headlight unit. Other changes were to a wider rear chain, roll-on feet for the centre stand and new hubs. These had ribbed, full-width, cast-iron drums housing 7 in. brakes

and were a group design seen on Triumph as well as other BSA models.

The finish was altered with much of the machine in black, and just the petrol and oil tanks, mudguards and toolbox to offset this in colour with almond-green for the B31 and gunmetal grey for the B33. The all-black option remained for both machines, but they were now nearing the end of their useful life.

The firm was beginning to move to lighter, unit-construction singles, since the market for large, easy running engines was fast fading. The two models were continued for 1959 but at the end of that year the B31 was dropped. The B33 had minor alterations for 1960, but it too was dropped before that

Nice restoration of a 1947 B32, which was based firmly on the road machine. The changes were minimal but included the ones really needed, such as tyres and exhaust system.

year was out, to bring the B range road models to their end.

Prospects

Road B models are traditional English singles from a time when that meant heavy flywheels, soft valve timing and a leisurely manner of progress from an easy flow of power. The machines were never fast, but speed was not what they were meant for. Buyers put their money down for reliable, no-nonsense motorcycles that took them to work and play, year-in, year-out without fail . . . which is what the machines did.

All are basically easy to work on and spares are less of a problem than for most, thanks to two factors. One is that the engines changed little over the lifetime of the machines; the other is the number of wearing parts common with the M20. This opens up the vast ex-service stock still in existence nearly half a century after the close of World War II.

The B models are pleasant to ride and cover the road quite quickly thanks to good handling, comfort and decent brakes. They are not for the motorway, interstate or autobahn, but for the byways and the main arterial roads of their time when the by-pass was none too common.

They rate three stars, for they are middle-of-the-road machines, neither spectacular nor lacking in interest. The colour finish is perhaps preferred to the early black and silver but the distinction is fine. Equally so are the various types with rigid, plunger or pivoted fork, for all have their adherents. Perhaps the final alternator models are less favoured but by a fine margin, while the one exception to the rating would be a machine with the alloy engine option. So rare is this that a cross-check on the factory records or copy of the original registration should be called for as proof that the ensemble is indeed genuine.

Competition B models

The first of the competition B models was the 348 cc B32 which appeared in January 1946 and was based on the road B31. The engine, gearbox, frame and forks were the same, but a sporting appearance was obtained by suitable changes to the equipment.

Thus, a high-level exhaust pipe and silencer were fitted along with competition tyres with a 21 in. front wheel and 4.00 in. rear tyre section. Sports type, chrome-plated mudguards were fitted and the plating was extended to the rear chainguard and brake backplates to give a bright shine to a dull and austere period. The model had its gearing lowered to suit its intended use, a crankcase shield was added and came with the mag-dyno and headlamp as standard. Optional was a magneto and battery lighting to special order; in those days it was normal practice to ride the machine to an event, so lights were needed on the way home.

In April 1947 the 499 cc B34 was created by fitting the larger engine into the same set of competition cycle parts, with the gearing adjusted to suit. The speedometer remained in the petrol tank as on the road models and copied them in moving to the top of the forks for 1948. At the same time a folding kick-start lever appeared and was no doubt retro-fitted to most of the earlier machines.

The 1948 finish was even brighter than before with the colour options of the road models being supplied as standard, so the tank panels and rim centres were Brunswick green for the B32 and Devon red for the B34. In addition there was an option of the chaincase being chrome plated, with this becoming standard the next year.

The year 1949 also brought in a revised gearbox, in line with the road models, and

The competition B32 and B34 of 1954 had a duplex rigid frame and all-alloy engine as they were built purely for trials use. There were no lights and only a small petrol tank.

the option of plunger rear suspension. It also saw the introduction of the B32 scrambles special in rigid or plunger forms which were simply the stock machine minus the road equipment and fitted with the right engine internals and tyres. They were listed only for that one year, as they were superseded by the Gold Star in scrambles form from 1950.

That year saw the B32 and B34 continue as they were but with two engine options in place of the standard all-iron unit. One was an all-alloy replica and the other the Gold Star unit. This was also all-alloy and used the same barrel but only the same cylinder head on the trials 350 version, as there was a different head on the 500. Thus, the 348 cc alloy and Gold Star engines were nearly identical but the 499 cc models had different crankcases.

The Gold Star engine option was dropped at the end of 1951, but the alloy option continued for 1952 when a dualseat became an option. From 1953 the wheel rims were chrome plated and the models returned to their earlier sparkle, after the dreary period of restrictions in 1952 when they had to adopt all-matt silver tanks and rims.

For 1954 the two competition models were revised with the alloy engine being fitted as standard. The plunger frame was dropped and, as standard, the machines used a new duplex rigid frame. With this went an alloy chaincase and small alloy petrol tank, but the other details were much as before. A

This is the 1957 model, the final year for the B34. It was sold in the USA as the Clipper with pivoted-fork frame and central oil tank.

magneto was fitted but no dynamo, as the machines were built solely for trials use and came with the silencer tilted up, saddle and the parts generally tucked in.

They were also available with the pivoted fork frame and the road front forks with the headlamp cowl, although the B34 stuck to its 7 in. front brake. They kept the chrome-plated mudguards and rear chainguard in line with their sporting image, but used some details such as the oil tank from the road machines.

This situation continued for 1955 at the end of which the rigid models were dropped. The two remaining models adopted a central oil tank for 1956 and changed to Amal Monobloc carburettors the following year. By this time the trials world was moving on and the day of the larger capacity four-stroke was coming to an end. BSA had other ideas for a smaller, lighter machine, so the B32 and B34 were quietly dropped from the range at the end of 1957.

Prospects

Four stars for all competition B models as original machines are now quite rare, and all qualify for pre-65 trials. How suitable they are is another matter, for the early machines are really too long, low and heavy, although the later ones with alloy engines were much improved.

Any machine with an option has a plus, but may need checking with even more care than usual. Many competition machines of that era led a hard and varied life and often were used on the roads during the week as well as for a trial on the weekend. It was a short step to the odd outing on the grass or a local scramble, with the suitable removal and addition of selected parts.

Often, machines would be modified in both large and small ways to make them more suited to the owner, so they need a thorough check if you are seeking an original example. Be especially wary of any claims that a Gold Star engine has been fitted or that the machine is an ex-works one. The first calls for the special engine number with the letters GS in it in the right place, and the second is seldom true. Even when it is, do not expect anything too special; most factory goodies were removed before such models were sold off. More often they were broken up, with some parts possibly being used for new products.

A genuine ex-works machine with full documented proof would rate five stars, but beware—all that glistens is not gold and such machines are generally known and counted. Anything that appears without a history is likely to be spurious and could well be an amalgam of road and trial parts. Avoid them unless you need only the parts and the price for them alone is right.

Gold Star

The manner in which the original Gold Star won its spurs and name has already been described along with its lukewarm prewar reception. During this brief period it moved from sports to fast tourer but failed to find much favour with the public. When the name was revived late in 1948 it was for a rather different machine which was to make its mark in most branches of the sport, and become a legend, one of the great cult machines of all time.

The postwar model first appeared as the 348 cc B32 Gold Star with an all-alloy engine in the plunger frame and much as the standard B32. What set it off was the bench-tested engine and the range of options that enabled it to be prepared for any form of sporting event, from a local trial to the Clubman's TT.

The engine was the major change from the B32, due to the alloy top half with the pushrod tunnel cast in head and barrel. The design had its origins in the prewar iron B29 and alloy versions of this built by the factory

The first postwar Gold Star was based on the 348 cc engine. This one is in 1949 Clubman's TT guise so there are no electrics or silencer. The riding position leaves something to be desired.

for competition use just after the war. From this came the concept of a machine suitable for the Clubman, and with it enough options to cope with trials, scrambles, grass-track and road racing.

The options covered the engine internals such as compression ratio, cams, carburettor and exhaust system, while there was one cylinder head for the trials specification and another for all the rest. Other options were for gearbox ratios, gearing, tank size, tyres and whether the machine had lights or not with either a magneto or mag-dyno.

The Gold Star was first shown as a sports model with full road equipment but in the B32 finish with plenty of chrome plating. The tank had matt silver panels and special Gold Star badges, and the model kept to the competition tyre sizes as standard.

For the Clubman's TT of that time, much of the road equipment could be discarded so the detailed option list covered this aspect. Surprisingly, the machine could run in the race without silencer, dynamo or lamps, so the list included an extension piece to fit on the standard exhaust pipe. The model went on to dominate the Clubman's series in time, especially the 350 cc class which it won consistently from 1949 to 1956. The later 500 cc model took longer to get on top of the opposition, but in the end you had to have a Gold Star to win. This domination was one of the factors that led to the race series being dropped.

The other versions were, at first, just as popular, and during 1949 the 499 cc B34 Gold Star joined the smaller model. While similar to the 350 in many ways, and based on the B34 with an alloy top half, it also had a revised crankcase and main bearing design.

Both sizes were known as the ZB version in time, as these letters were part of the engine prefix. All genuine Gold Stars included the letters GS in the identification on the engine case, so a typical number would begin as ZB32GS, followed by a serial number. Without this form of marking the engine is suspect; care is needed to not confuse the all-alloy competition engines with the Gold Star.

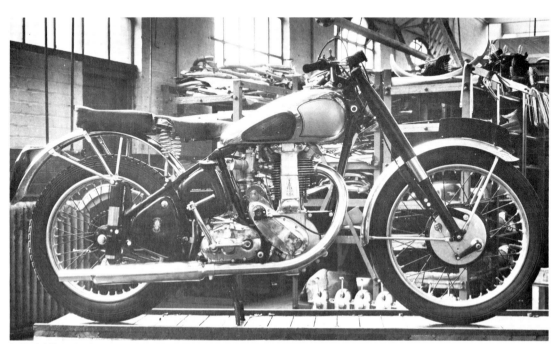

A Gold Star being prepared for the 1951 Clubman's TT, showing its all-alloy engine, reversed gear pedal, saddle, pillion pad and standard plunger frame.

For 1950 both models were fitted with the 8 in. front brake, except when built to the trials or scrambles specification which kept the 7 in. In this form they continued for 1951 until late in that year when the top half of the 499 cc engine was modified. The parts became diecast, and to help with this the rocker box was separated from the cylinder head proper so the construction differed. The barrel was much as before and the head continued to be held by the four long crankcase fixings plus four more short bolts running up into it.

The 348 cc engine followed suit in April 1952, and with the new top half went a shorter connecting rod to reduce the engine height. There were also many detail changes to keep the machines competitive in both classes, and there was the option of a dual-seat.

For 1953 the existing engines went into a new frame with pivoted fork rear suspension and in this form became known as the BB models. This was the frame used by the road B range the next year, with minor changes and a revised gearbox with the

The 1952 Gold Star engine. The revised cylinder head had a separate rocker box and extra fins on the pushrod tunnel.

A B34 499 cc Gold Star prepared for the 1952 International Six Days Trial with the small-fin engine in the pivoted-fork frame that was soon adopted by the whole large-capacity range.

choice of internal ratios expanded. The model range was also extended with one for ISDT use, appearing with a suitable combination of the many options available.

The Gold Star cycle parts were to change little from then on, but the engines still had further development stages awaiting them. Thus, for 1954, the Clubman and road racing versions had a new engine type known as the CB while the others kept to the BB style.

The CB engine had far more finning on both head and barrel than before plus a sweptback exhaust pipe, so the machine appearance was strikingly different. Inside there was an even shorter connecting rod and, for the 500, oval flywheels to ensure the piston skirt kept clear of them at all times. The crankshaft was strengthened and the valve gaps were set with eccentric rockers, while engine breathing was improved by a timed rotary valve driven by the magneto gear. An Amal GP carburettor provided the mixture with a feed from a flexibly mounted remote float chamber. Controls were fitted to clip-ons with welded-on lever pivots.

Both the BB and CB models continued into 1955 but not with the ISDT version. They were joined by the DB models which used the CB cycle parts with little change and similar engines. These had a much improved oil feed to the crankshaft and, for the 350 only, a revised barrel with much thicker liner. Fins appeared on the vented front brake drum, and the silencer was rather special and designed to work with the Clubman cams and timing.

At the end of the year the BB and CB versions were dropped along with the trials models to leave the DB types which continued and were joined by one final model. This was the 499 cc DBD which was built only in that capacity and differed from the DB in having a 1½ in. Amal GP, the largest available, and a silencer with tapered front section. Two new options appeared in the form of a five-gallon alloy tank and the famous full-width 190 mm front brake.

The DBD was the final development of the Gold Star and in Clubman form the most desirable—both then and now. At the end of 1956 the touring or road specification was

The first production Gold Star with the pivoted-fork frame was the BB version of 1953. Here it is in road or touring form, which continued for two more years.

A 1955 Gold Star when both CB and DB versions were built in both engine sizes and various forms to suit road, track or off-road use.

The DB Gold Star with big-finned engine as offered to the USA market for 1957. The high rise bars would be completely out of place in its home country.

dropped and a year later the road racing models went the same way along with the DB version and thus the 350. This left just the DBD Clubman and scrambles models for 1958 in the same form with minor alterations.

For 1959 the DB32 returned but in the form of a 500 fitted with the smaller engine, and the scrambles version in either size was fitted with a central oil tank. The Gold Star

continued in this manner into the 1960s but its days were by then numbered. The 350 was built only to special order from 1960, and while it ran on to 1962 there were few made in that final year.

The DBD34 remained for one more year in both versions to the end, which had become inevitable. The model was far from competitive in road racing, the Clubman's TT was a fond memory and the two-stroke

The final version of the scrambles model of the Gold Star in 1961. It was little altered and stayed like this to the end.

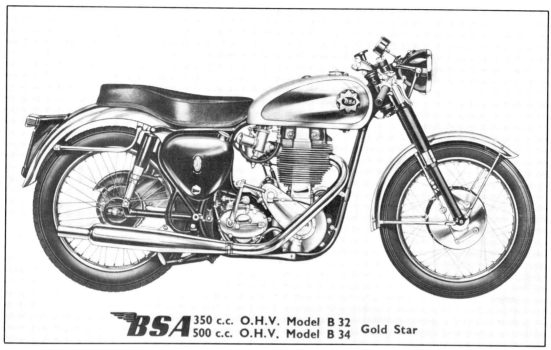

BSA 350 c.c. O.H.V. Model B 32
500 c.c. O.H.V. Model B 34 Gold Star

The most desirable of the whole lot is the late type Clubman Gold Star which was built as the DB32. It is preferred in DBD34 guise with sweptback exhaust and tapered silencer.

had taken over for scrambles. In addition, supplies of the Lucas mag-dyno had dried up and the firm was moving on to unit construction.

Prospects

All Gold Star models are desirable, collectable and one of the best investments, so five stars all round but especially for the DBD model in Clubman trim. Other models and versions may be even less common but it is the DBD with its clip-ons, twin instruments, ultra-close ratio gearbox and silencer that makes a twittering noise on the overrun which is the classic.

In original trim with massive Grand Prix carburettor the Gold Stars can be a problem to start and reluctant to tick over, so they are commonly fitted with a Concentric. This makes them much easier to live with on the road, and it is no problem to revert to the GP for shows while also not wearing out this fine carburettor.

Besides all that, the Gold Star is also a nice sporting motorcycle to use. It has perfor-

mance, handling and brakes so, aside from motorways, gives an enjoyable if noisy ride. Definitely one to take pleasure from.

Drive side of a restored Gold Star showing the typical BSA primary chaincase and toolbox. Racing seat on this one but still fitted with horn and dynamo.

44

Fine restoration of a Gold Star complete with
full-width front brake and all the right gear in the
most desirable Clubman form.

Chapter 4

Pre-unit plodders

★★	C10, rigid	1945–53
★★	C10, plunger	1951–53
★★	C10, four-speed	1951–53
★★	C10, plunger, four-speed	1951–53
★★	C11, rigid	1945–53
★★	C11 de luxe	1948–51
★★	C11, plunger	1951–53
★★	C11, four-speed	1951–53
★★	C11, plunger, four-speed	1951–53
★★	C10L, plunger	1954–55
★★	C10L, plunger, four-speed	1956–57
★★	C11G, rigid	1954
★★	C11G, plunger	1954–55
★★	C11G, plunger, four-speed	1954–55
★★	C12, swing arm	1956–58
★★	M20, rigid	1945–55
★★	M20, plunger	1951–55
★★★	M21, rigid	1946–60
★★★	M21, plunger	1951–63
★★★	M33, rigid	1948–55
★★★	M33, plunger	1951–57

As well as the cheeky Bantam for beginners, the touring ohv singles, the twins and the sporting models, BSA made some humdrum machines for riding to work on and for pulling a sidecar. Most had a side-valve engine and this class often included their smallest four-stroke.

Some are disparagingly called "grey porridge," but such epithets are hardly deserved, for they filled a need at the time. They had to run to and from work everyday without fail, be easy to repair and cheap to buy. Economy in petrol was expected, so it was really too much to expect such machines to offer much in the way of performance.

For a working man with a two- or three-mile journey to the factory, often in heavy traffic, quick, sure and easy starting was the prime consideration since the journey lasted only a few minutes anyway. Being able to pick up spares from any one of a hundred outlets and fitting them on the kitchen table was another.

BSA as a company was only too aware of this in the 1930s, and when its dry-sump single range was laid down in 1937 it included some side-valve models both large and small. Among them were the 496 cc M20 and 596 cc M21, both with side-valve engines and quite similar except in capacity.

Both were rugged machines with a sturdy bottom half (adopted by the B range after the war), heavyweight gearbox and a massive frame well able to withstand the stresses of sidecar work. Their construction was simi-lar to that of the smaller models, simply stronger and heavier.

Such machines seldom saw many changes, other than to the tank finish and badge, but by 1940 had at least progressed to foot-change for the gearbox. This made them eminently suitable for the army and thus the M20 joined up for the duration in large numbers. Heavy and lumbering it might have been, but it was tough enough to withstand army use.

Before this the M20 and M21 were joined by new 249 cc lightweights which took over the bottom end of the range with cheaper machines. The first was the side-valve C10 which was introduced in 1938 and was much simplified compared with the B models it replaced.

The C10 engine was the traditional English design reduced to a minimum with iron head and barrel. The crankshaft was built up with roller big end and ran in one ball race and one bush. It drove the camshaft with a gear pair and the oil pump with a worm, while the camshaft carried a skew gear and

Bottom of the 1946 range was the C10, often sneered at as grey porridge, but for all that able to do a useful job in those difficult postwar years of acute shortage.

sprocket at one end. The first drove the cam in the points housing mounted external to the timing cover while the second drove the dynamo. This was clamped to the rear of the crankcase and rotated to adjust drive chain tension.

This simple engine was fed by a small Amal carburettor and exhausted into a tubular silencer carried low down on the right. It drove a three-speed gearbox with handchange, and both items were fitted into a simple diamond frame with bolted-on rear subframe. Light girders went at the front and carried both headlamp and speedometer, while both wheels had offset hubs with small drum brakes. A saddle and toolbox were provided, and the petrol and oil tanks were combined into one with twin fillers, side by side.

For 1939 the basic C10 was joined by a de luxe version with footchange and the C11 with overhead valves. This was similar to the side-valve unit, with the valve gear extended up through tunnels in the iron head and barrel. The pushrods crossed over within it so lay at the same angle as the valves, with the rockers positioned across the engine to suit. A single alloy cover

enclosed both and gave ready access to their adjusters. The C11 had footchange as standard but in other respects was the same as the C10, except for the use of 20 in. wheels rather than 19 in.

The two models were intended to continue for 1940 and be joined by a larger 348 cc machine with side-valve engine and listed as the C12. It used many C10 parts so was hard to distinguish from it, and only a few were made. With the outbreak of war the C range went out of production except for

Companion to the C10 was the overhead-valve C11, which shared nearly all parts except the engine top half, but including the girder forks, used until April 1946.

some training C10 machines and one batch of the C11 for Indian service.

Postwar C range

The postwar C range picked up in 1945 more or less where it had left off six years earlier. Only the C10 and C11 were offered in basic form, with the footchange gearbox and still with girder forks. There were minor

For 1954 the older models were replaced by new ones with an alternator. This is the C11G overhead-valve machine, available with three or four speeds and plunger or rigid frame.

detail changes, but the major one was to a separate oil tank in the traditional English position, under the saddle and on the right.

Because of this the petrol tank was new and had only one filler cap, while the oil lines and their connections to the crankcase were revised. The finish was in black with the tank chrome plated with matt silver panels— a smart, albeit somewhat austere look to match the times.

In April 1946 the two models were fitted with telescopic front forks of typical BSA design with hydraulic damping and the speedometer moved into the tank top. For 1948 a C11 de luxe joined the other two machines and proved popular, with a nice finish of blue tank panels and wheel rim centres. It brightened the scene and sold well, for it combined everyday utility with better performance than the C10 offered.

The side-valve engine was given an alloy cylinder head for 1949, and the ohv had deeper fins for 1951. That year also introduced options of plunger rear suspension and a four-speed gearbox for both models; these usually went together but not always. The exception was for the de luxe model which, in its final year, was either rigid with three or plunger with four speeds.

The matching side-valve 249 cc model was the C10L, which used a number of Bantam parts to

keep the weight and price low. Only built in the plunger frame but with the choice of speeds.

The C11 changed to 19 in. wheels for 1952, and the next year the speedometer on it and the C10 finally moved out of the tank top to a much more sensible position on the fork crown. There was also a dualseat option for the C11, the last year of the two machines.

Both were replaced for 1954 by models with an alternator on the left end of the crankshaft, and the points cam and its auto-advance on the end of the camshaft. In this form the side-valve model became the C10L and the ohv the C11G but, except for the electrics, the engines were essentially as before but with a new timed breather.

The C10L was built with a three-speed gearbox and had a lighter frame than before, with plunger rear suspension based on Bantam parts. The telescopic front forks also came from the Bantam and were the stronger D3 type, with a cowl to support the headlamp. The hubs were from the Bantam too and the finish a nice two-tone green.

The C11G retained the C11 frame in rigid or plunger forms with the four-speed gearbox available only for the latter. It was finished in maroon, as had been the last year of the C11, and had similar brakes to the C10L. The front proved rather inadequate so was changed to a 7 in. for 1955 when the machine was listed only with the plunger frame and both models were fitted with a Monobloc carburettor.

There was further revision for 1956 when the C10L was fitted with a new four-speed gearbox and its plunger frame modified to accept this. At the same time more fins appeared on the cylinder head and the wiring was simplified by fitting separate switches for lights and ignition. In this form it continued to the end of 1957 when it was dropped from the range.

For 1956 the C11G was replaced by the C12 which did however retain its engine. This went into a new frame which kept the open diamond form, although fitted with

For 1956 the overhead-valve engine went into a pivoted-fork frame with a new four-speed gearbox, and became the C12.

pivoted fork rear suspension. It thus continued to rely on the engine and gearbox plates for its rigidity.

The C12 used the new four-speed gearbox, and a pressing filled in the gap between it and the engine. In other respects, the machine followed expected lines with telescopic front forks, dualseat with the oil tank beneath it and drum brakes. These went into full-width hubs and the front continued at its 7 in. size. Less usual was a switch panel on the right side, aft of the oil tank and up in the subframe corner, but this simplified the wiring to some extent.

The C12 continued in this form to offer a good compromise of speed and economy to the daily rider who sought value for the money. With the BSA spares systems of the time it served its purpose well.

Prospects

Two stars all the way down the list for C range models, as these are not machines that are collected. Most people prefer the larger capacity B range and certainly not sidevalves, except to be perverse to some degree.

Performance is not highly rated, and these small four-strokes are just as hard and

expensive to restore as any other. Therefore the market concentrates on size and glamour and the grey porridge fades away.

This might just bring its own revolution in the long term with the simple, cheap and common becoming rare and valuable. Thus, there possibly could be an eventual hedge—especially for the C10 which tended to be bought, ridden to death and thrown away.

If bought just to ride, remember the period brakes. But expect a pleasant trip down memory lane at a placid rate, economy you have always dreamed of and handling you may rather forget. These C range machines have a charm of their own and if that attracts you, accept it and ignore the comments.

Postwar M range

When the war ended, BSA carried on building the M20 but in its civilian finish of black with a lined silver tank. The changes were minimal so it was still the 496 cc sidevalve engine, four-speed gearbox with footchange, rugged rigid frame, girder forks and saddle.

Although the M20 was normally thought of as a sidecar machine, it was at that time

The postwar M range picked up where it left off with the M20, still with its girder forks and just as used by thousands of servicemen except for the colour and odd details.

available with a solo frame which lacked the sidecar lugs—a curious anomaly for such a weighty model at a time when production stability was a top priority and options anathema in the factory. It was most likely a way of using up stocks of the military frame (which lacked the lugs) to save cost and vanished after 1947.

Before then, early in 1946, the M20 was joined by the M21 whose capacity had changed to 591 cc back in 1938. This made it a long-stroke version of the smaller model, with a common bore size but not piston. In all other respects it was the same machine as the M20 with a fatter rear tyre and raised gear ratios.

Due to the shortages then prevalent both models had to manage without footrest rubbers at first, but the military serrated rests proved adequate until the rubbers appeared during 1947. There were few other changes then, but for 1948 the two machines were joined by a third listed as the M33. This used the frame and cycle parts from the M21 with a 499 cc ohv B33 engine installed in place of the side-valve. The finish was brightened up with chrome plating on the tank and rims, with this becoming an option for the side-valve machines.

The result was a machine that gave the sidecar driver more performance, especially acceleration, while retaining the strength to deal with sidecar loads. This philosophy was, however, dealt a blow in June 1948 when all three models changed over to telescopic front forks, which most sidecar owners viewed as a retrograde step. The extra front wheel movement brought it, and its mudguard, too close to the frame downtube for comfort, so this was pulled back a little and lost its straight line from headstock to engine plates.

Having given the M range the heavyweight forks from the B models, the two combined to use one common gearbox for 1949. There were no changes for 1950, but 1951 brought light alloy cylinder heads for the side-valve engines and the option of plunger rear suspension for all models. This was as for the B range, so even more details became common across the larger models of the range.

There was a dualseat option for 1952 and the next year brought the headlamp cowl common to the road B range. All three models ran on as they were for 1954, but with round plastic tank badges, and 1955 saw the introduction of Monobloc carburettors and

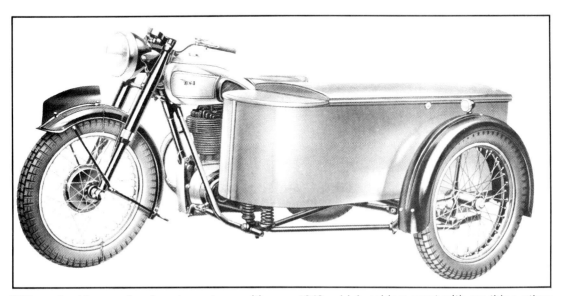

BSA made sidecars of various types to go with their range of machines; this is the box chair of 1949, which seldom went with anything other than a side-valve single.

a steering lock. At the end of the year the M20 was dropped, as the market for a plodding side-valve single was shrinking fast, and the M33 continued only in plunger frame form.

The two remaining M range models were given an 8 in. front brake for 1956 along with a valanced front mudguard, but at the end of 1957 the M33 was dropped. The M21 continued, mainly for service use, and lost its headlamp cowl in 1958 while from 1959 it was by special order only. The year 1960 saw the last rigid frame machine and a year later

some AA models had an alternator added to boost the generated charge.

By this time the supply of magnetos was drying up and those that could be obtained could be used more profitably on a Gold Star, while the market for the M21 was fast vanishing. A combination of these factors led to the model's demise in 1963 to bring the long running side-valve line to an end.

Years later the classic bike revival and interest in military machines brought the M range back into some favour. It had an advantage of a truly enormous spares stock

The M20 and M21 as sold in 1954 when still available in rigid or plunger form with an old specification that continued to be called for.

For 1955 the finish of the M20 and M21 was little altered. This is the version with plunger rear suspension, which was all that was offered from the next year on.

The M33 was first built in 1948 and combined the M range cycle parts with the B33 engine to

produce a sidecar-hauling machine with a touch more sparkle. This is the final 1957 version.

from its army days, with parts still in their crates nearly half a century after they were packed. This was especially helpful to the military enthusiast but also of great assistance to all M model owners, and for owners of other BSA ranges with common parts.

Prospects

Two stars for the M20 and three for the other M range machines, which are preferred because of capacity or the overhead valves. There is little to distinguish the rigid from the plunger or girder from telescopics, although an M33 with girders has to be a rare bird.

The M20 is less popular, as there were so many built for the army, but is becoming more valuable with modern riders appreciating the charms of those big, heavy flywheels. In addition to the standard models there are those supplied to the services and the AA for which there is a small demand but only for original specification. Such machines bring variety to the scene and often remembrance of a long-ago breakdown, and the help that dealt with it.

These models may be found with a sidecar attached which is a plus if contemporary. A single adult chair works well with any machine without dragging the performance down and is more appropriate than a massive double adult body. And don't forget the box sidecar used by the AA, a fitting companion to a side-valve model with both finished in bright yellow with the club badge on display.

The M range is a pleasant and relaxing series to ride in solo form or with a third wheel; not for those in a hurry, but for those taking time to see the countryside.

Chapter 5

Unit singles

★★	C15 Star	1959–67
★★★★	C15S	1959–65
★★★★	C15T	1959–65
★★	SS80	1961–65
★★	C15 Sportsman	1966
★★★	C15 Pastoral	1963–65
★★★	C15 Starfire Roadster	1963–65
★★★	C15 Trials Cat	1965
★★	C25 Barracuda	1967
★	B25 Starfire	1968–70
★★	B25 Fleetstar	1969
★	B25SS	1971
★	B25T	1971
★★	B40	1961–67
★★	SS90	1962–65
★★	B40E	1964–65
★★★★	B44GP	1965–67
★★	B44VE	1966–67
★★	B44VS	1967–70
★★★	B44VR	1967
★★★	B44SS	1968–70
★	B50SS	1971–72
★	B50T	1971–72
★★	B50MX	1971–73

BSA introduced their unit-construction single for the 1959 season to replace the aging C12 and showed it as a new design. In truth, the engine was based on the Triumph 200 cc Cub which in turn came from the 150 cc Terrier of the early 1950s. Thus the C15, as the new model was called, inherited both strengths and weaknesses even though the detail parts were all new.

The aim was to provide a simple, reliable workhorse for the novice or young rider with clean, attractive lines and the minimum of controls or fuss. It was also intended to use the design as the basis of competition models and a larger capacity to fill the place of the elderly B31 and B33. In time this was to happen, but the various models never seemed to achieve that solid dependability that the BSA name had stood for and prospered from.

Road unit models

The launch machine was the C15 Star with a simple 247 cc engine built in unit with a four-speed gearbox and fitted to a frame with cycle parts in the current group style. Thus, the forks had the same form of nacelle as the twins, and the hubs were similar but smaller.

The engine unit had a central, vertical crankcase split line with the gearbox shell incorporated in the right half and the chaincase inner in the left. The crankshaft ran in one ball race and one bush, and was of pressed-up construction with a plain big end

for the one-piece connecting rod. This was bushed at the small end, and the gudgeon pin held a conventional three-ring piston giving a compression ratio of 7.25:1.

The piston ran in a simple iron barrel which spigoted down into the crankcase and up into the alloy head. This had a detachable rocker box with access covers and the valves were restrained by duplex springs. They were opened by cams on a single shaft directly geared to the crankshaft with tappets and pushrods to transfer their motion to the rockers, with a chrome-plated pushrod tube between head and crankcase.

The crankshaft also had a skew gear on the right to drive a shaft which ran down to a duplex gear oil pump and up to a points housing. The first was a typical BSA unit for the dry-sump system, while the second included the advance mechanism for the ignition timing.

At the other end of the crankshaft there was an alternator, and inboard of that the duplex primary chain. This drove a multi-plate clutch with shock absorber centre

BSA 250 O H V model C 15

The start of a long line that was to stretch to a full 500 cc in time. This is the 1958 C15, which began it but had its roots in the past and the Triumph Terrier and Cub.

which in turn passed the drive to the conventional gearbox. The gears were selected using a quadrant camplate mounted in front of them, and the change mechanism terminated in a pedal on the right.

The gearbox had an end cover on the right which extended forward to also enclose the timing gears. The kickstart spring went outside this and a further cover, with star embellishment, ran the length of the engine to conceal this. It all made for a neat, compact unit.

This went into a simple loop frame with twin rails beneath the engine and a bolted-on subframe. It had pivoted fork rear suspension and the lines of the D7 Bantam, albeit on a heavier scale. At the front went

For 1961 the unit single was enlarged to 343 cc to produce the B40 and went into similar cycle parts but with larger wheels and front brake.

During 1961 the SS80 appeared with a tuned C15 engine and more chrome to tempt the young learner buyers, restricted in the UK to 250 cc at that time.

It came as no great surprise that a sports version of the B40 should appear as the SS90. It duly did this during 1962.

hydraulically damped telescopic forks which were modelled on the lines of those fitted to others in the range. They had a similar nacelle to carry the headlight and also the instruments and switches, with a well-valanced front mudguard to keep the dirt at bay.

Both wheels had full-width, cast-iron hubs in line with other models, but with single leading shoe brakes of only 6 in. size. The wheel diameter was 17 in. and the rear mudguard was as well valanced as the front. The machine had a dualseat fitted as standard, and the petrol tank carried pear-shaped plastic badges.

The oil tank went on the right under the dualseat nose and was matched on the left by a toolbox. The two were joined by a centre panel that carried the ignition switch and the air filter for the Amal Monobloc which supplied the mixture. The battery went behind the filter with access from the toolbox side, and the exhaust system went low down on the right with a tubular silencer.

The finish that first year was fuchsia red or turquoise green for the petrol and oil tanks, mudguards, toolbox and centre panel, which gave the machine a smart appearance.

It then ran with few changes for some years other than to the finish, which in time became red with an option of blue and sometimes all-black. Otherwise, there was a new ignition switch with key for 1962, and a roller big end bearing and primary chain tensioner for 1964.

Before then the C15 had been joined by two further models for 1961, the first was the B40 with bored-out 343 cc engine. This was much the same in many areas but was easy to spot as the pushrods ran up in a tunnel cast in the barrel rather than in a separate tube. The wheel size was increased to 18 in., and a 7 in. front brake was specified but of the same type with the full-width hub. The finish was royal red without any options.

The second new model was the SS80 which did not appear until April 1961 and was a sports version of the C15. It had a tuned engine with roller big end and a primary chain tensioner, while the gearbox had closer ratios than the standard model. Little on the cycle side was altered, so there were 17 in. wheels and 6 in. brakes; the petrol tank was larger at three gallons, as was that on the B40.

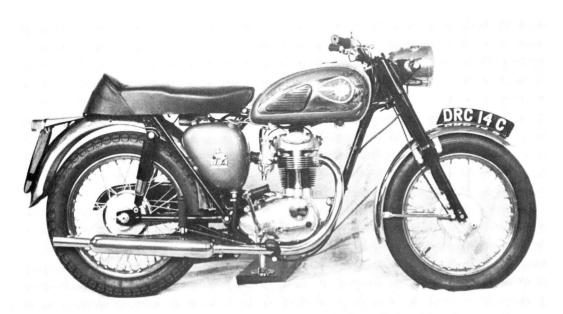

For 1966 the C15 Sportsman replaced the SS80 and gained a humped seat and separate head-lamp shell to distinguish it from earlier machines.

For 1962 the B40 was fitted with the roller big end and primary chain tensioner as well as the new ignition switch. In May it was joined by the SS90 which was a sports version on the same lines as the 247 cc model. It differed in having chrome-plated mudguards fitted as standard rather than as an option as for the smaller model, and was finished in red with the SS80 in blue or all-black.

The 247 cc BSA single was revamped for 1967 into the C25 Barracuda, which had much revised engine internals and a fresh style with square fins for the head and barrel.

The unit single was stretched further to 441 cc for 1967; the result used the C25 cycle parts to create the B44VR Victor Roadster. Both offered similar performance in different ways.

All four models continued as they were for 1963, but for 1964 the C15 was finally fitted with the roller big end and primary chain tensioner. All were modified for 1965 when the points were moved into the timing cover where their cam was driven from the camshaft. At the same time a rack and pinion mechanism was adopted for lifting the clutch, and inside there was a revised gearbox.

This was all rather late in the day, however, for both sports models were dropped at the end of the year. The C15 continued for 1966 while the SS80 was replaced by the C15 Sportsman, which had a separate headlamp shell and a dualseat with a hump. In July, both models had the engine bottom half revised to use a competition developed type with stronger crankcase and ball and roller main bearings. There were many other detail internal improvements which made these late engines much better than earlier examples. The B40 was not included in the 1966 brochure, but some were made that year and the next with the modified engine bottom half from mid-1966.

Just the C15 and B40 continued for 1967, their final year, for the Sportsman was replaced by the C25 Barracuda. This was a super sports machine which kept to the C15 engine layout but was different internally and in looks. The top half was new with an alloy barrel and both it and the head had extensive square finning. The pushrod tunnel went in the barrel, so the external tube was no longer needed.

Inside there was a one-piece forged crankshaft which had two separate flywheels pressed on and then bolted in place. This design meant a split big end for the alloy rod, and shell bearings were used to run on the crankpin. The specification was fierce with high compression ratio, large carburettor and hot cams, which gave the bearings a hard time. Eccentric rocker spindle adjustment was a new feature as was the Concentric carburettor.

The frame was based on a trail version of the C15 and had a welded subframe but otherwise followed the original lines. It had better support for the rear fork as there were twin seat tubes, and the front forks were of an improved design. The wheels had 18 in. rims and 7 in. brakes in offset hubs, with the rear one reverting to the old crinkle hub design. The petrol tank was in fibreglass, as was the left side panel, and the oil tank was shaped to match the sculptured panel form.

The Barracuda was sold in the United States as the B25 Starfire and joined by a larger model known as the B44VR Victor Roadster. This had a 441 cc version of the engine with the same square-fin engine style, although inside it there was a built-up crankshaft with roller big end. Externally it was as the C25, and both had twelve-volt electrics and a bright finish with chrome-plated mudguards and Bushfire orange tanks and side cover.

For 1968 the smaller model was sold only as the B25 Starfire and was given a full-width front hub while the larger machine became the B44SS. It too went to the same type of front hub but larger with an 8 in. brake, while the finishes changed to Nutley

blue for the B25 and peony red for the larger model now known as the Shooting Star.

Both models continued for 1969 with changes to a 7 in. twin leading shoe front brake, steel petrol tank and the option of a rev-counter. They were joined by the B25 Fleetstar which was an economy model designed for fleet use with a detuned engine and less ornate finish. Its softer engine tune made it more reliable and it is preferred by many as being less likely to give trouble in daily use.

The Fleetstar was offered only for the one year, so the other models ran on for 1970 by themselves with minor alterations. At the end of the year they were discontinued and replaced as part of the major revamp for 1971.

The new range was intended to take BSA on into the decade but was short-lived, for the company was already in serious financial trouble. This was not helped by the extensive redesigning or the common use of major

By 1969 the 250 was the B25 Starfire with the twin leading shoe front brake as used by other group models at that time.

subassemblies by both BSA and Triumph and, in some cases, badge engineering of the same models for the two marques. This was to alienate enthusiasts for both models who preferred their make to be special and different from any other.

The 1970 Starfire had become a high performance and rather fragile machine, but one whose problems can be overcome with some work and careful assembly.

The new road singles were the B25SS and B50SS street scramblers which were also given the old Gold Star name, to the great annoyance of many BSA owners and riders. Such were the depths the company had sunk to.

Both models had many common parts and the frame was one. It carried the engine oil in its single top and downtubes, with duplex ones under and behind the engine unit. The rear fork pivoted on needle rollers, with these and their spindle able to move in frame plates to set the rear chain tension. Both frame and fork were finished in a grey paint which looked shabby even when spotlessly clean.

At the front went new slimline forks without the benefit of gaiters to protect the stanchions or seals. The wheels had conical hubs so the rear was no longer quickly and easily detachable, and the front hub had an 8 in. twin leading shoe brake. This had an air-scoop and internal cams for adjustment, but its twin cam levers were too short to be

The larger single in 1970 was the B44SS Shooting Star, which continued to offer a more relaxed ride than the B25 but still responded well to care and attention.

effective so it failed to match its promise. For export the B25SS was fitted with a single leading shoe 6 in. front brake but the larger model kept its bigger brake for all markets.

The smaller engine was the B25 unit as before but the larger one was the final development of the original Terrier concept by the factory; it found more life as the CCM in later years. The B50SS engine was stretched out to 499 cc and had a built-up crankshaft with a needle roller big end bearing. It ran in one further main bearing than before, with this installed on the left to help support the primary drive. Otherwise, the larger engine copied the smaller just as it did with the cycle parts. Both models had an exhaust pipe that wound tortuously along the engine and inside the frame to a lozenge-shaped silencer. This was fitted with a heat shield, but the system itself was finished in matt black.

BSA dropped the B25SS at the end of 1971 and continued with just the B50SS as part of a depleted range for 1972. At the end of that year the road single was dropped for good, as were just about everything else. It was the end of a long run.

Prospects

Not many stars for the road unit collection; the bikes have a bad reputation for oil leaks, short big-end life, engine blowups and vibration. These claims are not unwarranted, for the engine unit has weak areas. But remember that the 250s were often bought by novices and could expect a hard life.

BSA should have recognized this and dealt with the problems, but they did not, hence the reputation. This means, then, that if the engine is put together properly, if use is made of specialist knowledge, if the highly tuned models are avoided and if the machine is used sympathetically there is some hope at the end of the tunnel for these road units.

Thus, here we have a series that is not regarded well at all, so prices can be reasonable but still offer acceptable transport. It can also allow for some switching of pistons and cams to help increase reliability while keeping the external sports appearance, all of which can be considered fun but not an investment, so it does not have to be at all serious.

The singles had a major revamp for 1971 but this B25SS Gold Star used a revered name and was supposed to be a street scrambler; it was only listed for one year.

The new-style single was also enlarged to a full 499 cc as the B50SS Gold Star with some engine revisions to the bottom half. One went well in some long distance races.

Ratings of two stars go to the C15, SS80 and C15 Sportsman, with something of a plus for the later models with revised big end and a minus for the SS80 with its tendency to fly apart. The same for the B40 and SS90 with the same proviso, and also two for the Barracuda, not because it is a nice machine but because it was the first revamped model and built only for one year.

The B25 sinks to one star except for the softer tuned Fleetstar version, and the final 1971 version keeps to this low level or less. The 441 cc machines may climb to three stars on the basis of their capacity and less stressful performance, a marginal rating followed by a descent to the depths of one star for the B50SS. This does in fact have the makings of a good machine as shown by its successes in endurance racing, but is not a favoured model. If you like the idea, can find one and can sort it out, this could be a pleasant ride which just might be tomorrow's long shot.

Off-road unit models

Once the basic C15 was launched and in production, BSA turned their attention to the off-road scene and early in 1959 introduced the C15T for trials and C15S for scrambles. The works trials machine had first been seen in 1957 but had not received much comment even though the road model was not then on sale.

The road unit single was turned into a pair of competition models soon after it was launched; this is the C15S as built for scrambles in 1961.

The Military B40M was built in 1967 after the standard model had been dropped. It combined the virtues of two off-road models to produce what was wanted.

The early competition variants were based strongly on the road C15, with the frame essentially the same with some minor alterations. The forks were similar but with different yokes, legs and stanchions, while stock hubs were used but laced into new rims. The front was a 20 in. with a 3.00 in. tyre section, but the rears differed. The trials model had a 4.00x18 in. tyre while the scrambles one used 3.50x19 in., so the rims were to suit.

The mudguards were painted with the option of chrome plating, the fuel tank was smaller than standard and an undershield and short seat were fitted. The exhaust system was upswept with no silencer for the scrambler, which also had ball end control levers.

The engines were modified internally with respect to compression ratio, camshaft and gearbox ratios, with wide and close respectively for trials and scrambles. Both suffered by being fitted with the dreadful Lucas energy transfer ignition system, which de-

Jeff Smith with his works BSA on which he was extremely successful and from which came the Victor Grand Prix scrambler.

pended totally on the points opening at the right time. This had to refer to the maximum flux of the alternator and had no hope with all the gears, including a skew pair, between the two.

The addition of an auto-advance made matters worse, even when its movement was restricted, and the result was an engine that would start but not run or run but not start. Bad for scrambles and impossible for trials, with its call for dead slow and full throttle riding in the space of a few yards. The points gap and timing proved to be ultra-critical so any wear in the points drive was also fatal to the system.

Undeterred, BSA continued with the two models with little alteration until 1962 when both were given the roller big end and primary chain tensioner, and the scrambles model adopted the rear tyre size of the trials model. In May that year they had further changes with alloy petrol tank and mudguards plus a 7 in. front brake in an offset hub. The scrambles model was also fitted with strutted bars and an expansion chamber formed in the end of its open exhaust pipe.

The two models were further revised for 1963 with a new frame with duplex seat tubes. This allowed the exhaust system to run inside the seat and subframe tubes to be better tucked in. At the same time a central oil tank was adopted along with a revised air filter.

This is the B44VS Victor Special from 1968 when it was an export-only model for trail use, hence the undershield, tucked-in exhaust and suitable tyres.

Two more models were added to the range as the C15 Pastoral and C15 Starfire Roadster, both for export only and using a combination of competition and road parts. The Pastoral had the engine from the C15T and most of the same cycle parts but with the road petrol tank, silencer and handlebars along with the short dualseat. It had a taillight and speedometer so was a daytime trail machine.

The Starfire Roadster approached the matter in another way by using a stock C15 engine in the full set of competition cycle parts. The engine was modified a little in subsequent years, but the concept remained unaltered.

The four off-road models became five for 1964 when they were joined by the B40E Enduro Star, again an export-only machine. This copied the Starfire Roadster and used the same competition cycle parts with a mildly modified B40 engine to produce the same form of off-road model with a little more power.

The five became seven for 1965 and all had the points moved into the timing cover which at least gave the energy transfer ignition some hope. They also gained the rack and pinion clutch mechanism and had the gearbox revised. One of the new models was the C15 Trials Cat which was really a C15T minus the headlamp for daytime trail riding, so it used the same set of competition cycle parts and engine.

The second new machine was something different and the start of a new engine line. It was the 441 cc B44GP Grand Prix built solely for scrambles. With this in view, it had a special frame that carried the engine oil, the older pattern of offset hubs with the rear crinkle design, special front forks and a well-tuned engine. This had the new crankcase with ball and roller main bearings that was later adopted by the road models. The bottom half supported an alloy cylinder with hard-chrome-plated bore in which ran a high compression piston. The cylinder head was modified to suit the enlarged engine size and the degree of tuning it received, while the camshaft had racing timing.

There were major changes at the end of 1965 for all the C15 variants, and the B40E was dropped. Only the B44GP went forward for 1966. It was joined by the B44VE Victor Enduro which used the GP engine but in detuned form with a linered barrel. This went into the C15 competition frame with lights to produce an enduro or trail model.

For 1967 the B44GP was given a 7 in. rear brake, as was the B44VE which also had a Concentric carburettor. For both it was their last year, and they were joined by the B44VS Victor Special which was a trail version of the Roadster. It retained the humped dualseat and had a small headlight, undershield and upswept, tucked-in exhaust system to suit its intended use. Sports mudguards and trail tyres on wheels with offset hubs completed the model which was finished off with a polished alloy petrol tank with bright yellow side panels.

Only the Victor Special continued into 1968 when it was given an 8 in. front brake, while for the next year it had the option of a rev-counter. Its final year was 1970 when it had some detail improvements after which it was dropped in favour of the 1971 new-model line-up.

In 1971, the off-road models were much as the road models with 247 or 499 cc engines. The trail models were the B25T and B50T Victor Trail, and both were little different to the road-going Gold Star versions. They kept to the 20 in. front wheel size, and both used the 6 in. front brake. The front mudguard was bolted to the underside of the fork crown so was sprung, unlike the road model. There were also strutted handlebars, but the lights including the indicators were the same.

A third off-road model lined up with the other two for 1971 and this was the B50MX Victor Moto-Cross built solely for scrambles. It had a suitably tuned engine in a similar frame with common forks and wheels, with minor adaptations for racing. The exhaust was either as on the later form of the C15S or the one pipe fed into two silencers mounted one above the other on the right of the machine. Rather odd to say the least, but done to hold down the noise of those big 500 cc bangs to an acceptable level.

None of the new range had much of a life and the off-road models were no exception.

The 250 was the first to go, so only the larger models ran into 1972 and only the scrambles model to 1973. Then it was all over for BSA, although the B50MX did resurface in 1974 as the TR5MX, wearing Triumph badges. This design led to the CCM scramblers.

Prospects

A variable scene was presented by these off-road unit models, one partly affected by the pre-65 events, the crucial year. At a stroke, that removes all the models with the points in the timing cover and with the stronger Victor bottom end, leaving bad electrics and a weak engine.

Fortunately, some of this can be rectified by using modern systems without losing the original looks, so the C15S and C15T models are popular ones. Four stars for them for this reason, and four for the Grand Prix Victor simply because it is such a special model.

The C15 Pastoral rates a three but is seldom seen in its own country. Neither are the C15 Trials Cat or Starfire Roadster, while all three represent various ways of achieving a rather similar object. They are all on the pre-65 borderline, and while not true trials models could be adapted to some extent.

The B40E is a similar machine but rates only two stars as the bigger engine was not as good at finding grip as the smaller. This is generally thought to be a matter of flywheel weight restricted by the 250 crankcase. Even so, it is a machine that is quite adequate for loafing along the trails, and is another sold mainly for export.

Next we have the Victors Enduro and Special which date from 1966, which is a drawback. The larger capacity and stronger bottom end are redeeming features but they are not popular models, generally export only, and fail to fit the scene well. As such they are a good buy as a trail hack if you like them, but no more.

The B50MX rates two stars as the final development of the line with the potential to run well and strongly. Otherwise it falls outside the true classic scene and has limited appeal as it is a pure scrambles model.

The B25T and B50T Trail rate just one star each as their styling won them few converts then or now. They suffer from the same snags and strengths as the road models, so have few friends and are in fact quite rare in their home country. If you just want something for gentle trail riding they could have merit, but only if assembled correctly and perhaps detuned a little.

Ownership

Most of the unit singles have problem areas of some sort, with many due to combination of the original stretched design, poor detail work and a rev-happy novice at the controls. However, answers to most of the

troubles have been developed by specialists of the model, so it is possible to build a nice, reliable unit-construction BSA single.

If you do this it will be more for your own use and pleasure than as an investment, so it will be worth doing only if you intend to keep the machine for some time. Some detuning could be worth doing as well, as the result is likely to be a nicer ride and more reliable machine to boot. It could pay also to keep full records of all the work done for when it comes time to sell.

The first problem for many engines is the ignition, with the energy transfer setup the

The revamped models of 1971 included this B50T Victor Trail, much as the road machine other than the front mudguard, brake and bars.

The third new 1971 model with the 499 cc engine was this B50MX Victor Moto-Cross ma-chine, which was more the business and was built for three seasons.

worst culprit. The answer is to move on to a modern electronic arrangement powered by the battery or the alternator. This will greatly improve matters and should make starting easier.

The next area of concern is the lubrication system with its crude filter and doubtful alloy pump body. This pump body can easily distort and cause the pump to leak or its gears to seize, but a replacement with iron body is available. The next step to improve matters is to add a better filter in the return line with a screw-on car-type cartridge. Oil leaks are less easy to cure due to the narrow joint faces in some places, but careful work to flatten them plus good gaskets and no excess of jointing compound will improve matters no end.

The general health of the later 250 engine will be improved by using an 8:1 piston rather than the high ratio one originally specified. These engines tended to suffer badly at the hands of owners so need to be viewed with this in mind and any slightly suspect components replaced.

Vibration can be due to worn mounting holes in both crankcase and frame plates, but the first can be sleeved and the second welded and redrilled. This can make quite an improvement. The gearbox may jump out of gear but this can be dealt with using shims, and there is a replacement for the weak kick-start quadrant. Note that the B50 connecting rod has been known to break which usually destroys the engine. The cause is not known, but there is a rod from the CCM that can be used and does not fracture.

Deal with these and the result can be a good engine that will offer acceptable performance without any problems. Otherwise, the unit single can be something of a hazard to your wallet.

Chapter 6

Pre-unit twins

★★★	495 A7, rigid	1947–50
★★★	495 A7, plunger	1949–50
★★★	497 A7, rigid	1951
★★★	497 A7, plunger	1951–54
★★★	497 A7, swing arm	1954–62
★★★★	495 A7ST Star Twin, plunger	1949–50
★★★★	497 A7ST Star Twin, plunger	1951–54
★★★★	497 A7SS Shooting Star	1954–62
★★★	646 A10, rigid	1950–51
★★★	646 A10, plunger	1950–57
★★★	646 A10, swing arm	1954–63
★★★★★	646 A10SF Super Flash	1953–54
★★★★	646 A10RR Road Rocket	1954–57
★★★★	646 A10SR Super Rocket	1958–63
★★★★★	646 A10RS Rocket Scrambler	1958–59
★★★★★	646 A10S Spitfire	1960–63
★★★★★	646 A10RGS Rocket Gold Star	1962–63

BSA entered the vertical twin market late in 1946 with a machine that was typical of its way of thought and action. There was nothing too far removed from convention in nearly all areas, and the design of the cycle parts followed the lines already laid down by the B and M singles. The crankshaft and centre stand did break new ground, but both were to be revised back to tradition in the first few months of production.

The postwar twin was not their first look at that type of machine, for BSA, like the

First of the postwar BSA twin line was the A7. It is seen here as in 1946 when it was launched with the speedometer in the petrol tank top, then a common BSA feature.

rest of the industry, had been impressed by the sales of the Triumph Speed Twin introduced late in 1937, and wanted to join the trend. Unfortunately for BSA, the war broke out before they could bring the new design into production.

During the war BSA did some work on a military machine with a side-valve vertical twin engine, but before the war they got as far as building two prototypes. These came in the 1938–39 period and one was of 350 cc with overhead valves. The other was more interesting, with 500 cc and an overhead camshaft. This was driven by shaft and bevels on the right and looked a worthy contender for the sports machine market. Both used contemporary cycle parts and were not to be seen again.

After the war BSA concentrated at first on getting the singles back into production, but it was not long before the twin was announced.

Pre-unit twins

The new twin was announced in September 1946 as the A7, but the basic layout of the engine had been mentioned in the press early in 1945 as a BSA patent. It was the form that the twins were to use for some thirty years, with only detail alterations to suit changes in capacity and general engine development.

The engine was something of a long stroke with its dimensions of 62x82 mm, giving a capacity of 495 cc. Construction followed conventional lines in most respects, so the alloy crankcase was split on its vertical centre line with a one-piece cast-iron block bolted to it with separate cylinder head. The one unusual feature of the crankcase was that it was designed so that the gearbox could be bolted to it rather than mounted separately in plates.

The crankshaft was unusual in its construction but assembled to provide the conventional 360 degree layout demanded by the stock magneto, with its equally spaced firing intervals. Otherwise, a 180 degree crankshaft, coil ignition and twin carburettors would have been needed and this was just not considered to be the thing for such a model. The main bearings were a ball race on the drive side and a bush on the timing one.

There were three sections to the crankshaft with each outer part fixing to a central flywheel. The outers each comprised a half-shaft, web and crankpin forged as one, and thus were able to accommodate a one-piece connecting rod. With these assembled, the tapered extension of each crankpin could then be fitted to a matching taper in the flywheel. The two outers were then drawn together by a special locking bolt. This had a differential thread which meant that there were two threads, one for each part, and their pitch differed. The effect was that each turn of the bolt only clamped the parts up by the pitch difference to produce a high clamping force with threads of normal section and strength.

This design was used for the first 500 engines but was then changed to a more normal arrangement with a one-piece forged crankshaft, bolted-on flywheel and split connecting rods. The latter were steel stampings with shell bearings and a bushed small end and so were easy to service. They ran up

A 1948 A7 in Singapore. This early engine had a rather long stroke and other features which were not to last too long.

to flat top pistons with three rings, two compression and one oil; the pistons were held by fully floating hollow gudgeon pins retained by wire circlips.

The pistons ran in an iron block bolted to the crankcase and this had a tunnel cast up the back for the pushrods. The cylinder head was also a one-piece iron casting, but the rocker boxes were separate. The head had wells for the valves with a passage in each for the pushrods, twin parallel inlet ports and splayed exhaust ports. A copper and asbestos gasket went between head and block with nine bolts holding them together, the centre one of which lay at a slight angle. Thus it was always the first removed and last fitted.

Each pair of rockers was mounted in an alloy box bolted to the head over the valve well and pivoted on a long spindle. This ran right across the box, and during 1947 the exhaust spindle was drilled for an oil feed from the return line. The boxes were tied to each other with short straps and each had

BSA twin modified to run in the 1949 Scottish Six Days Trial while undergoing War Depart-ment tests. Machine based on works twin used by Bill Nicholson and ridden by N. J. Jarrett.

two access caps to enable the valve gaps to be set.

The valves were closed by duplex coil springs retained by split cotters and worked in cast-iron guides. They were opened by a single camshaft, which ran across the rear of the crankcase at a high level to move tappets running in guides mounted in the crankcase. Pushrods ran up from them to the rockers, and the inlet and exhaust were of different lengths and the rockers of different form and handed to suit the valve mechanism geometry. This design allowed the pushrod tunnel to be separated from the main block, which promoted good airflow and equal cooling for the cylinders.

The camshaft was gear driven with one intermediate gear between it and the crankshaft pinion, and this geartrain was continued on to the rear-mounted magneto with auto-advance. The intermediate gear had its spindle extended to an outer timing chest, and a sprocket mounted on its end drove the dynamo by chain. This chain ran in its own chamber within the case, and the dynamo itself was clamped to the front of the crankcase so that its rotation adjusted the chain tension.

A dry-sump lubrication system was used, with the duplex gear pump driven by a worm threaded on the end of the crankshaft. The oil tank was externally mounted under the saddle on the right of the machine and connected to the engine with feed and return pipes. The engine had a timed rotary breather which was driven by a stud screwed into the camshaft gear and housed in the inner timing cover, with suitable passages from the crankcase to the outside.

Carburation was by a single type 6 Amal with separate float chamber and the mixture was passed into an alloy manifold connected to the inlet ports. A drip shield was fitted between the mixing chamber and manifold to avoid fuel falling onto the magneto, and an air filter was fitted as standard with its

The A10 Golden Flash in 1951, a year after it appeared, based on the A7 but with a great deal of detail redesigning. Here in the plunger frame and with its lovely beige finish.

For 1951 the A7 was changed to copy the A10 engine so that many detail parts became com-mon to both models including nearly all the cycle parts.

Another A10 in 1951 when it was popular with young and old, for solo or sidecar use and in rigid or plunger frames.

housing squeezed between the oil tank and battery carrier. On the exhaust side went simple pipes which pushed into the ports and carried finned collars. They ran down low on each side to tubular silencers.

The engine drove the clutch via a duplex chain with a shock absorber built into the engine sprocket. The chain was tensioned with a slipper under its lower run, and this was set with a bolt in the underside of the chaincase. The inner part of the chaincase was formed as part of the left crankcase casting and the outer was another casting, polished and held in place by a run of small screws. The clutch was a multi-plate type clamped up by six coil springs and designed to run dry, so the whole assembly was enclosed by a domed pressing held to the clutch drum by a dozen screws.

The arrangement of the primary drive came about due to the fixed centres of the engine and gearbox, with these bolted together. The gearbox shell was similar to others made by BSA except that it included a large, square flange at the front which mated with four studs in the back of the crankcase. Due to this it could be removed only after the clutch had been dismantled to allow the gearbox to slide back past the inner chaincase.

The gearbox itself was conventional with four speeds, both clutch and final-drive sprockets on the left and the sleeve gear concentric with the mainshaft. The positive stop change mechanism with its foot pedal went on the right as did the kickstart lever, while the gearbox also provided the speedometer drive.

The assembled engine and gearbox unit was housed in a rigid frame built up from tubes brazed into forged lugs. There were single top and seat tubes, but duplex downtubes that ran back under the engine to the rear fork ends. Sidecar lugs were provided in the frame, and the first 1,000 had a telescopic centre stand.

This stand comprised a single tube that was fitted inside the frame seat tube, a substantial foot at its lower end and a compression spring arranged to hold the stand up. One side of the tube carried a series of ratchet grooves so that a pawl could lock into them and hold the stand down. On releasing the pawl the stand retracted.

Unfortunately this design, patented with the name of Edward Turner who was much better known for his work with Triumph, had its snags. One was that it failed to lift either wheel clear of the ground unless the machine itself was raised while a foot was kept on the stand base. In addition, a spring attachment failure could allow the stand to fall to the ground while riding, and any interference with the pawl lever when parked was likely to result in the machine falling over. During 1947 the idea was dropped and a normal hinged centre stand replaced it.

Front suspension was by telescopic forks and at first these carried a quickly detachable wheel that could interchange with the rear one. Both hubs were of the BSA crinkle pattern that allowed straight spokes to be used, and both connected to offset hubs with 7 in. brakes and were spoked to 19 in. rims.

Most of the cycle parts followed the lines of the heavier BSA singles with sound, func-

The original A7 Star Twin had appeared in 1949 using the old engine with twin carburettors but the later version managed with one Amal. This 1952 example has the economy finish of that era with no chrome plating on the tank.

tional mudguards, triangular toolbox set between the right chainstays, rear lifting handle and saddle. The electrics were Lucas with the ammeter and light switch set in a small panel in the rear of the headlamp shell. Less usual, although not for BSA at that time, was the location of the speedometer in the petrol tank top.

The finish was in Devon red or black for all painted parts, with the petrol tank chrome plated with lined panels. The wheel rims were plated with lined centres to match and there was a restrained amount of chrome plating of minor parts.

The A7 was an immediate success and its only real change for 1948 was to move the speedometer out of the tank and onto the top of the front forks. Rather more happened for 1949 when the model became available with the option of plunger rear suspension and was joined by a sports ver-

sion listed as the A7ST Star Twin. This had the sprung frame as standard, and both models had a new one-piece front hub that still allowed the front wheel to be removed easily.

The Star Twin engine was much as that of the A7 except for a rise in compression ratio and the fitting of twin carburettors. This raised the power a little, but in other respects the machines were virtually the same. Both had the rocker oil feed extended to the inlet side and a higher output dynamo, while the rigid frame became a two-part construction that bolted together. This allowed the front section to be used for the plunger frame as well, with alternative rear sections. The plungers themselves were as used by the B range of singles, with load and rebound springs under covers but without damping.

The two 495 cc models continued as they were for 1950 when they were joined by one

One of the three BSA Star Twins used for the successful 1952 Maudes trophy ride; it is under-going restoration in this photo. Nicely done and now on show in England.

of the best-loved BSA models, the A10 Golden Flash. This was of 646 cc, and this increase in capacity came to meet the needs of the export market with its clamour for more power. Within the fuel limitations of that time, the easiest route to more power was a larger engine, and both BSA and Triumph introduced these late in 1949.

The A10 engine was not simply an enlarged A7 but a development of it, with changes to most of the major parts and minor details. Relatively few of the old parts would fit the new engine, although the design was to the same layout and the looks similar. The remainder of the machine was the same in most areas, although there were improvements plus features which went only on the A10.

The Golden Flash was offered in rigid or plunger frame builds, and its engine retained the earlier layout of crankshaft, gear-driven camshaft and magneto, chain drive to dynamo, iron head, iron block and bolted-on gearbox. The rocker box was revised and became a one-piece item with two covers for access to the rocker ends for setting the valve gaps. This made assembly rather more difficult, as all four pushrods had to engage with the rockers at once. BSA offered a comb plate to help with this.

The cylinder head was now cast complete with the inlet manifold which had a small degree of downdraught, but the rocker gear was as before. The block followed the earlier pattern but had an extra hold-down stud, and was modified so that the tappets ran

For 1953 the BSA twins, including this Star Twin, adopted a headlamp cowl, with the ammeter and light switch set in its sides, but kept the semi-unit construction of engine and gearbox.

directly in it. They were arranged in pairs and had retainers to prevent them falling out when the block was raised during dismantling.

The pistons were designed for quiet running and had concave crowns as the compression ratio was a low 6.5:1. They attached to forged alloy connecting rods with bushed small ends, and the crankshaft design copied that of the A7. Like that, it ran in a bush on the timing side but had a roller race on the drive side. The crankcase was amended around the tappets to simply clear the extended cylinder block with its tappet guides, and had a trough cast under the camshaft to retain oil for the benefit of the cams. Otherwise the bottom half was essentially the same with no real alterations.

The A7 in 1954 when it was built with semi-unit construction and plunger frame as here and also in the new pivoted-fork frame with engine and gearbox separate.

The transmission continued as it was with a new gear set, while the engine unit went into much the same cycle parts as before with little exception. Among the areas that did change were the front mudguard which gained deep valances to carry the registration number plate on each side, and the front brake which increased in size to 8 in. The toolbox shape was amended, and for export there was a large capacity petrol tank.

Golden Flash in the plunger frame in 1954 and destined to continue to be listed up to 1957 specifically for the sidecar man who did not trust pivoted fork rear suspension.

The most striking feature of the new model was its finish which for export was in polychromatic silver beige for all painted parts. The tank was chrome plated with red-lined beige panels and the wheel rims plated, painted and lined to match. The beige had a golden look to it which really made the machine stand out in those rather drab postwar days and naturally led to the Golden Flash name.

On the home market the finish was at first black and the machine was fitted with a smaller tank, but this situation did not last for long. Quickly, most A10s were finished in the beige, and had the larger tank while few were built with the rigid frame. Those that were tended to be in black.

The A10 was joined by revised versions of the A7 and A7ST for 1951, and for these the engines were altered to reduce the stroke. Many detail parts became common between the 646 cc and new 497 cc engines, with the variations being the expected ones concerning capacity. This simplified production and spares stocking, but it also means that the early A7 engine can be more of a problem to the restorer.

The revised Star Twin had to manage with only one carburettor, but did have a sports camshaft to enhance the power and the 8 in. front brake to hold it in check. Its black finish continued much as for the touring models, but the tank became matt silver with panels outlined in red during the nickel shortage of the early 1950s.

At the end of 1951 the rigid frame versions of the A7 and A10 were dropped, so plungers alone were offered for 1952. That year also brought a pre-focus headlamp which in turn dictated the fitment of the useless underslung pilot light. A dualseat was offered as an option and taken up by many, and there were the inevitable minor improvements.

More excitement arrived for 1953 with the appearance of a new model in the form of the export-only A10SF Super Flash. This had a tuned 646 cc engine fitted into its own version of the plunger frame, which gave it an exciting high-speed ride. The frame was known to weave quite well on fast, bumpy corners anyway, and the extra power was more than it could handle. It was given the 8 in. front brake to help control it, and this went on the A7 as well to make it a common fit to the twins. The other twins were given a headlamp cowl for 1953 but the Super Flash kept the earlier arrangement.

The lovely 1955 A7SS Shooting Star was for many the best of the twins, combining enough performance for all practical purposes on the roads of the times with style and comfort.

There was a good deal of change for 1954 with new sports models in a new frame, for BSA had been well aware that the plunger had its limitations. The new models were listed as the A7SS and A10RR but became better known as the Shooting Star and Road Rocket, with both for export only at first. Both had a frame with pivoted fork rear suspension, and this was also used by new editions of the A7 and A10, also for export only at first.

The four new models had many common parts and a revised engine and gearbox. No longer were these two assemblies bolted together, so the semi-unit construction became pre-unit. The gearbox was thus mounted separately in plates, and the cycle had much in common with the later B range singles.

The engines had the crankcase altered to remove the rear mounting flange and add lugs to match the plates, while the gearbox shell was as for the singles. The frame was as well, with duplex downtubes which ran back under the engine but without the kink in the right rail as found on the singles to clear their oil pump.

The other cycle parts were single-bolt fuel tank, oil tank tucked into the corner of the right subframe, matching toolbox on the left, common mudguards and a dualseat fitted as standard. A saddle was listed as an option and all except the Road Rocket had the forks with the headlamp cowl, the exception using the older, separate type as on the Super Flash.

The engines were similar, but the sports versions had suitable camshafts and light

The sports model with the 646 cc engine was the Road Rocket seen here in 1956 form with the full-width light-alloy hubs, which came from the Ariel range.

alloy cylinder heads. The A7SS had a separate inlet manifold, but the Road Rocket kept to the A10 style with integral tract. Inside there were more common parts than not, with many still as when introduced in 1950.

The finish had been amended for 1953, following the nickel shortage, to a style with a painted petrol tank with lined chrome-plated side panels. The colour remained black or beige for the A10, but maroon was adopted for the A7 and a two-tone green for the Star Twin. These continued for 1954 and were adopted for the pivoted fork A7 and A10 plus the A7SS. The A10RR kept mainly to black but with the tank in the same style as the others and with a colour choice of red, matt silver or green.

Another use for the 646 cc BSA engine was found for 1954, with this unit being fitted to the Ariel Huntmaster model from then on up to 1959. The two firms were in the same group so this was a good way of providing Ariel with a larger capacity twin, and the appearance of the engine was altered with changes to the timing cover. There were other modifications as well, with some hard to understand as they increased costs

without any real benefit. One that was useful and welcomed by Ariel owners was an access hole in the top of the rocker box which made assembly much easier.

Harder to understand was the move of the sump plate so that it was bolted solely to the right crankcase and not, as on the BSA, to both. To this end there was a new left crankcase, without plate flange, and a new right with a repositioned flange. The right case was also altered to suit the new timing cover

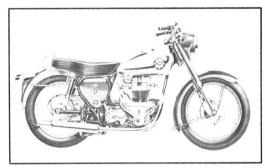

This is the A7SS Shooting Star in its USA form in 1957 when it was fitted with the usual high bars and rear handrail. This one also has the optional rev-counter drive on the timing chest.

The home-market Golden Flash of 1957 when it continued to offer enough performance with

comfort and the great BSA spares and service back-up.

shape, so there were new gaskets and parts made special for Ariel. Due to this it is important to check if your twin is fitted with an Ariel engine, as this will affect some of the spares. The majority of parts are as for the A10 but the engine number sequence is quite different.

For 1955 BSA clarified their twin-cylinder range by dropping the Star Twin, Super Flash and plunger A7 to leave five models. Four of these had pivoted fork frames with a tourer and sports version of each engine size, while the plunger A10 with semi-unit engine continued essentially for the sidecar driver. Otherwise, the underslung pilot light was replaced by one in the headlamp reflector, a steering lock was added to the front forks and a Monobloc carburettor appeared on all except the plunger A10 and Road Rocket.

The pre-unit twins did not change much further although there were alterations of some sort for most years. It was the wheels that received attention for 1956, when both were given full-width light alloy hubs with wide 7 in. brakes. These were as used by the road B singles and, like them, their operation

included a cross-shaft running in the rear fork pivot. A full rear chaincase was introduced as an option.

The plunger A10 alone continued with its offset 8 in. front brake but only for one more year, as it was dropped at the end of 1957 to leave the four basic models. They were joined for 1958 by the A10 Rocket Scrambler which was an export build used as much for off-road riding as scrambling. To this end it had open exhaust pipes, which both curled round to waist level on the left, no lights, and tyres, seat and mudguards to suit off-road use.

The 646 cc engine had been given a thicker block base flange and revised method of bolting the flywheel to the crankshaft for the Road Rocket in 1954. These features went onto the A10 engines for 1958 when the sports version became the A10SR or Super Rocket. All models had a new design of wheel hub and all except the A7 went back to an 8 in. front brake.

The new hubs were built up using pressings and a cast-iron drum to produce a full-width form also fitted to the road B range. They went with front forks with end caps

By 1958 all the twins used similar cycle parts, which included composite hubs built up from steel pressings and a cast-iron drum. This is the A7 for that year.

The A10 Rocket Scrambler which was built for 1958–59 and called for a great deal of strength as well as riding ability to hustle it along at any speed off-road.

which replaced the old screw-in spindle, and at the top a nacelle replaced the cowl to carry the light unit, instruments and switches. This nacelle was not used on the Rocket Scrambler or the export Super Rocket. The latter had a separate headlamp shell and speedometer head, with this often balanced by a matching rev-counter driven from the magneto gear. From 1958 all models had a revised finish with most of the painted parts in black and only the tanks, toolbox and mudguards in colour.

The Rocket Scrambler became the A10 Spitfire for 1960 when the Super Rocket rev-counter drive was taken from an extension of the oil pump driveshaft. The cable thus ran from the front of the inner timing cover, low down on the right, so was tucked in better than before. The machines were given pear-shaped tank badges and plain kneegrips which altered their looks but

retained the round badges for the smaller tank used for some export machines.

The pre-unit twins were now nearing the end of their days, for unit construction was fast approaching. However, the old design had one last, wonderful model to bring out

The drive side of the 1959 A10 with the lovely cast-alloy and well-polished primary chaincase used by all twins in one form or another.

and in 1962 it appeared as the fabulous A10RGS or Rocket Gold Star.

The idea of this model came from Gold Star specialist Eddie Dow whose Banbury firm built such a machine in the late 1950s. This was for a customer who simply wanted a Goldie with a twin engine, so this was constructed using stock parts. When the RGS finally appeared in 1962 it was some way removed from this concept, however. It used some Goldie parts, a Super Rocket engine and a number of details that were unique to it—which made nonsense of the concept somewhat, and makes restoration of an original RGS that much harder.

The engine was the Super Rocket twin with raised compression ratio, stock Monobloc carburettor and siamesed exhaust sys-tem with single silencer on the right. It was bench tested before installation and could also have a track silencer supplied, or the twin pipes and silencers of the Super Rocket as long as the rearset footrests were not in use.

The transmission was based on stock BSA parts but with close ratios in the gearbox with alternatives available. The pedal could fit to face forward or backward, and alternative camplates allowed this to be done while retaining the desired change direction. There were also different sizes of engine sprocket to enable the overall gearing to be altered.

The frame was special to the model and much as the Gold Star frame minus the right tube kink. The forks were also Gold Star with gaiters, so required the front wheels to

Happy couple of 1986 aboard their 1960 A10 Super Rocket, as the sports 646 cc twin had become. The nacelle was used from the model's first year of 1958.

have the screw-in spindle. This meant either an offset hub with 8 in. brake or the full-width alloy hub with the 190 mm brake. At the rear there was a 7 in. brake in an offset crinkle hub from the past.

The sports image was enhanced by handlebars that turned down and ball-end clutch and brake levers. Clip-on bars were an option, as was a rev-counter which sat beside the fork-mounted speedometer. The headlamp shell was supported by lugs on the chrome-plated fork sleeves. The same finish was applied to the mudguards, which were special to the model, while the tank was in silver with chrome panels lined in red.

All told, the Rocket Gold Star was quite a machine and one that was often imitated by a Super Rocket with options. This arose when that model had a rev-counter added and, to fit this, lost its nacelle and was fitted with the separate headlamp shell. With the optional plated mudguards plus downswept bars it was well on the way to the RGS in looks, although the hubs remained different.

The A10 Super Rocket of 1962 when it had but one more year to run. It was mourned when dropped as its successor lacked the style and fine lines of the pre-unit series.

Often these changes were made in the early 1960s to produce a café racer from the stock Super Rocket, and the change could run to varying degrees. The only way to be sure of starting from firm ground when buying is to work from the frame number which is fundamental. The engines were effectively the same while gearbox ratios, front forks, mudguards and other details can all be changed.

The Rocket Gold Star was the final form of the pre-unit BSA twin and only built for two years. For its 1963 season it was accompanied by the other three 646 cc models, but not the 497 cc ones which were dropped at the end of 1962. Some of the late A10 models were built with an alternator which meant a change to the primary chaincase, but before the end of 1963 all the models had been dropped.

Prospects

Never less than three stars for pre-unit twins, as these machines are big four-strokes and always manage to keep up with the market. They were also the preferred models, for the public never had the same affec-

Rebuilt Rocket Gold Star, the super sports twin built for just two short years and the pinnacle of the series. Very nice and in high demand.

tion for the later unit-construction twins.

Right at the top with five-plus stars has to be the Rocket Gold Star. This is the most desirable of the twins and a fine, fast motorcycle. Up there with it are two export-only machines that are rare indeed in their own country and normally seen only in the United States. These are the Super Flash and the off-road model sold first as the Rocket Scrambler and then as the Spitfire. Both were produced in small numbers and liable to updating changes, so original remaining examples must be few and far between.

The sports twins all must rate four stars, for they were some of the nicest machines produced by the British industry. The Shooting Star in particular has been highly rated by some of the most experienced riders around for its combination of assets. It is fast enough, has good acceleration, nice gearbox, smooth brakes and minimal vibration. All that adds up to comfort and a machine that can be ridden fast for a long time without aches or pains.

If the Shooting Star is the one to buy to ride, then the Road Rocket and later Super Rocket are equally desirable. Their extra capacity clinches the choice for them for many owners. The only real difference is the engine size, and to some riders the larger is preferred as it allows higher gearing and easier, more restful high-speed cruising. Usually this is so but in this case it has to be balanced against a touch more vibration and

a degree of harshness the A7SS seems to avoid. Still, nice motorcycles and as fine for riding as they are for owning.

The Star Twins also rate four stars for interest and rarity. The early long-stroke version was built only for two years so is seldom seen now, but the later one is a little easier to find. It has a nice engine, but cannot hope to offer the comfort or road-holding of the pivoted fork machines. Despite this it is desirable and a good ride within its limits.

The rest of the range qualified on three stars and is the touring A7 and A10 in their various forms. Some are more plentiful than others, which can affect their rating half a star one way or the other. The Devon red A7 and beige A10 always seem to be more in demand than the prosaic black ones.

The rigid frame is a rare bird while for riding, the pivoted fork is best. So choice and use both influence model rating. To some enthusiasts the first A10 in its plunger frame with the export tank and beige finish was the best of the lot, while others might look to other years.

As always, taste and needs are considerations as is use. The early long-stroke engines are known to run hot and spares for them are much harder to find, so they are not the best choice for regular or lengthy use. That aside, and with due deference to the variations in the cycle side, all the models offer sound, reliable transport from a basic good design.

Chapter 7

Unit twins

★★★	A50 Star	1962–65
★★★	A50R Royal Star	1966–70
★★★★	A50CC Cyclone Competition	1964–65
★★★★	A50C Cyclone Road (USA)	1965
★★★★	A50C Cyclone (UK)	1965
★★★★	A50CC Cyclone Clubman (UK)	1965
★★★★	A50W Wasp	1966–67
★★★	A65 Star	1962–65
★★★★	A65R Rocket	1964–65
★★★	A65T/R Thunderbolt Rocket	1964
★★★★	A65L/R Lightning Rocket	1964–65
★★★★	A65L Lightning	1965
★★★★	A65LC Lightning Clubman	1965
★★★★	A65SH Spitfire Hornet	1964–65
★★★	A65T Thunderbolt	1966–72
★★★★	A65L Lightning	1966–72
★★★★★	A65S Spitfire	1966–68
★★★★	A65H Hornet	1966–67
★★★★	A65FS Firebird Scrambler	1968–71
★★★★★	A70L Lightning	1972
★★★	T65 Thunderbolt	1973

At the start of January 1962, BSA announced a new pair of twins to replace the aging A7 and A10. In time, this was to extend to a model range and, in its final form, run into the 1970s and the last days of the company. With the new models came unit construction, less weight and rounder styling, but much of the engineering came from the old twins.

The new engine unit presented a smoother exterior to the world, and there were two capacities based on a common stroke with the smaller one of 499 cc for the A50 Star and the larger 654 cc twin for the A65 Star. Under the covers, much was as before with a 360 degree crankshaft, gear drive to the camshaft located high up in the crankcase, pushrods running up in a tunnel in the rear

The start of the unit-construction twin line was with just two models, the 499 cc A50, seen here, and the 654 cc A65, which shared the same cycle parts and most of the engine ones.

of the block and the same variety of rockers for the valve geometry.

There were also a good few new features from the start including an alloy head which had the rocker spindle lugs cast into it. This made assembly much easier, and when this was complete a simple cover was added to enclose the entire rocker and valve gear in the head. Both engines had a single Amal Monobloc carburettor to supply the mixture, and this bolted to an alloy manifold which fed the parallel inlet ports. The tappet design was simplified but they remained in their tunnel in the rear of the iron block, and the pushrods were in light alloy with hardened steel end caps.

The connecting rods were in light alloy and the crankshaft used the same design, with its flywheel retained by three bolts. It continued to run in a bush on the timing side but had a ball race for location on the drive side. The drives to the oil pump and camshaft were much as before, but in place of the magneto there was coil ignition. This was controlled by points set in the timing cover, and their cam and its auto-advance were driven by the intermediate gear.

The dynamo was replaced by an alternator fitted onto the left end of the crankshaft outboard of the triplex primary drive chain. This had a slipper tensioner on its underside and drove a multi-plate clutch hung on the mainshaft of the four-speed gearbox. This followed conventional lines, so the final-drive sprocket sat on the left just inboard of the clutch while the gear pedal went on the right.

The gearbox change mechanism was similar to that of the unit singles with a quadrant camplate to move the selectors. They, and the plate, were mounted on the gearbox inner cover along with both main and layshaft, each complete with its gears, so the assembly could be put together and then offered up to the gearbox housing as one.

The main crankcase casting was split along the vertical engine centre line with the gearbox chamber entirely contained in the right half and open on the right side to allow the assembly of gears and shafts to be fitted. This chamber was quite separate from the engine and had its own oil with appropriate filling, level and drain plugs.

The crankcase casting was continued to the right to an inner cover which ran the length of the engine, and under this went the timing gears and the gearbox inner plate complete with its assembled parts. These two areas were kept separate in the casting by an inner wall between them, and the front chamber contained the oil pump mounting face as well as the timing gears. The inner cover carried the points plate and a polished outer completed the enclosure and carried the points access cover.

The left casting extended back to match the right and form the inner primary chaincase. It was carried over the gearbox sprocket and access to this was provided with a large circular plate bolted to the inner chaincase section. This carried a seal to keep the dirt

The A65R Rocket twin introduced in 1964 and the first step from the touring twins. It had a tuned engine, siamesed exhaust, separate headlamp shell and more chrome plating.

One of the 1964 export models was this Spitfire Hornet for motocross and thus with tuned twin-carburettor engine, open exhausts and raised bars.

and grease at bay, but it had a hard life. The bottom half castings were completed by the polished chaincase outer which was attached with a ring of screws.

There was a new frame for the new engine units but along the lines of the past, with single top tube and duplex downtubes which ran round the engine and gearbox. The rear subframe was welded on and the rear fork and other frame details were much as in the BSA mould. There were typical marque forks at the front with a nacelle to carry the headlamp, instruments and switches, and a steering damper and lock were fitted.

The wheels had 18 in. rims spoked to full-width hubs of composite cast-iron and steel-pressing construction. They were thus similar to those used by others in the range, and had an 8 in. front brake for the A65 with a 7 in. for the A50 and both rears. Well-valanced mudguards were fitted front and rear, and

the clean lines were accentuated by large side covers. These filled in the whole of the subframe corner and extended forward to enclose the carburettor and its air cleaner. A lever was fitted to the float chamber to allow the tickler to be operated, while the air control was on the handlebars.

The seat, petrol tank and handlebars with their controls were typical BSA with a single-bolt fixing for the tank. The oil tank went on the right under the cover with the tools behind it and was matched by the battery on the left. The twin ignition coils sat just ahead and on either side of the air cleaner.

The machines were finished in black for most painted parts, but the mudguards, side covers and petrol tank were coloured with chrome-plated side panels for the tank. Colours were metallic green for the A50 and Nutley blue for the A65, with an all-black option for both and flamboyant red for the

A65 only. Other options included a full rear chaincase, legshields, prop stand, safety bars, handrail, rear carrier and whitewall tyres.

The two models ran on as they were for the next year and for 1964 the A65 had the option of twelve-volt electrics with zener diode control. At the same time a further five models were added to the range, with all but one for export only. The one that appeared on the home market was the A65R Rocket which had a tuned 654 cc engine with siamesed exhaust pipes, although the twin pipes remained an option.

The Rocket had chrome-plated fork sleeves supporting a separate headlamp shell in place of the nacelle, so the speedometer was mounted on a bracket attached to the fork top. A rev-counter was an option and, where fitted, the two instruments sat side by side on a common plate. The rev-counter drive came from the oil pump shaft with the inner timing cover amended for the cable attachment.

The forks had gaiters and a folding kickstart was fitted, this being an option for the Star models, while the mudguards lacked valances and were chrome plated. The finish for the petrol tank and side covers was similar to the other models but in flamboyant red.

Among the other four export models for 1964, the A65T/R Thunderbolt Rocket was the A65R in its US form. It had high handlebars and a smaller tank but was otherwise as for the home market. For those who craved the same but with more power, there was the A65L/R Lightning Rocket which had a new cylinder head with splayed inlet ports to carry twin carburettors. The side panels were abbreviated to clear these and their air cleaners, but essentially it was the same model as the Thunderbolt so had the raised bars and small tank.

The other two models were for off-road use and were the A50CC Cyclone Competition and A65SH Spitfire Hornet in the two capacities. Both had twin carburettors, open exhaust systems and no lights while the tyres, mudguards and undershield were to suit their intended use.

The A65T/R was dropped for 1965 as no one wanted the single carburettor when

they could have two. The rest of the range ran on with an 8 in. front brake for the A50 and an optional set of close-ratio gears for all models. They were joined by five more to bring the range of twins up to eleven.

One of the new machines was for export and listed as the A50C Cyclone Roadster. It was built on the same lines as the A65L/R with high bars and small tank but with the twin carburettor version of the 499 cc engine. It thus had the abbreviated side covers along with fork gaiters, chrome mudguards and separate headlamp shell.

The other four new twins were sports models in two forms and the two capacities. All had tuned engines with twin carburettors, and the first pair were the A50C

Also for export was this 1964 Lightning Rocket, which again had the twin carburettors but came with standard exhausts, small tank and raised bars.

For production racing in 1965 there was the Lightning Clubman, which came with all the right parts and could have a fairing as well. Also listed as the Cyclone Clubman with the 499 cc engine.

The 1965 export Cyclone Road machine with the 499 cc twin-carburettor engine, tank and bars expected for the times. Most buyers preferred 654 cc and thus the Lightning.

Special Lightning fitted with "rocket tubes" for a James Bond film. Rider is Chris Vincent who dominated UK sidecar racing for many years using BSA twins.

Cyclone and A65L Lightning. Both had a humped-back dualseat, separate chrome-plated headlamp shell, fork gaiters, rev-counter and folding kickstart lever to offer a fast road performance.

For those who sought something more, there were the A50CC Cyclone Clubman and A65LC Lightning Clubman which were set up for production machine racing. To this end they had downturned bars, siamesed exhaust, close-ratio gears, rearsets, racing seat and a metallic gold finish for the tank and side panels. There was also a list of options, with the 190 mm front brake in its full-width alloy hub one of them. Others included a five-gallon petrol tank in alloy or fibreglass, alloy rims, clip-ons, twin pipes and silencers, and a fibreglass fairing.

This added up to an impressive range of models but actually was quite excessive, so was drastically pruned and generally renamed for 1966. All models went over to twelve-volt electrics, two-way fork damping and a three-spring clutch. The range was reduced to just six machines, two of 499 cc and four of 654 cc.

The basic tourers were the A50R Royal Star and A65T Thunderbolt which were not far removed from the original 1962 models. The most noticeable change was the new fork which had gaiters and a separate, chrome-plated headlamp shell, while the mudguards were less valanced than before. The speedometer drive moved to the rear wheel and the finishes were flamboyant red and blue respectively.

There were two sports models for 1966, with the first the A65L Lightning much as the previous year except for the general improvements to the range. The second was the A65SS Spitfire Mk II which took the place of the Lightning Clubman with a highly tuned engine fitted with twin Amal Grand Prix carburettors. It used many of the Lightning cycle parts but had the 190 mm front brake and alloy rims as standard.

The final pair of models were the A50W Wasp and A65H Hornet built for off-road use, the Hornet for competition only with open, waist-level exhaust pipes. The Hornet engine was the same well-tuned one as used by the Spitfire but fitted with twin Monobloc carburettors complete with round air filters. The machine had off-road tyres, undershield and rev-counter with ignition from an energy transfer system, and the petrol was carried in a small fibreglass tank.

The Wasp was similar but had twin low-level exhaust pipes with silencers, a speedometer as well as a rev-counter, touring dualseat without hump and could thus be used on the road. The engine was the tuned version of the 499 cc unit with energy transfer ignition and again breathed through twin Monoblocs, with the fuel in a small fibreglass tank. Both Wasp and Hornet were without lights in true American street scrambler form, and were finished in sapphire blue and flamboyant red respectively for the tank and side covers.

All six models went forward for 1967 with the Spitfire becoming the Mk III. The engines were fitted with a finned rocker box lid and gained an access cover to the rotor in the

The off-road 499 cc Wasp twin of 1966 with its functional looks but enough weight to make riding hard work at times.

chaincase. The Spitfire alone changed to twin Concentric carburettors, and the option of a five-gallon tank introduced during 1966 continued along with a small, two-gallon tank for the United States and a four-gallon for the home market. All models now had the humped-back dualseat and even the tourers fitted the blade section rear mudguard.

The range of twins dropped to five for 1968 with the Wasp no longer included. The Spitfire was listed as the Mk IV, and the 654 cc off-road model was called the A65FS Firebird Scrambler. All now had Concentric carburettors, and the three sports 650s had a twin leading shoe front brake. This went into an 8 in. full-width hub and the cable swept in from the rear to connect to the straight cam lever at the front.

The Firebird Scrambler was similar to the old Hornet with regard to the engine but more like the Wasp in specification. Thus, it was fitted with lights and silencers as standard with the exhaust pipes run at waist level on each side. The model was therefore street legal, widening its appeal in the United States.

The road models had a new diecast alloy tank badge that year, and all were built in the export form with high-rise bars and side reflectors. Low bars continued to be listed and fitted for most home market owners, while the Spitfire and Lightning alone lost their lower rear unit shrouds.

At the end of the year the Spitfire was replaced by the triple, so there were only

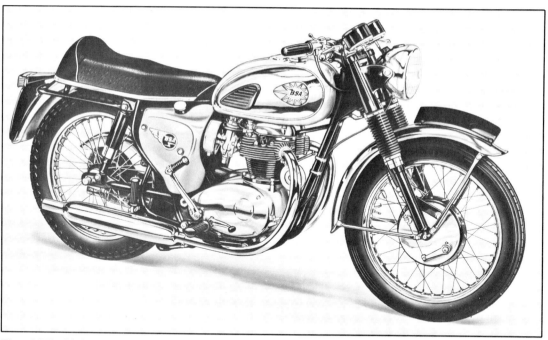

The A65L Lightning twin for 1966 when it offered a great deal of performance with good handling but marginal brakes in a stylish and popular package.

The Mk III version of the BSA Spitfire as in 1967 when it no longer breathed through twin Amal GP carburettors but was still a fragile engine.

four twins for 1969. All now had the 8 in. brake in the full-width hub, but its twin leading shoes had a new bellcrank lever for the front cam which allowed the cable to run down the fork leg. All had a more powerful alternator and a number of minor changes which included no covers at all for the rear units, and exhaust balance pipes for the 650s but not the Royal Star. The Firebird Scrambler pipes were moved to the left with one above the other, plus a mesh grille to keep the rider's leg clear of the twin silencers. There were twin horns for the Lightning alone.

Little changed for 1970 on any of the four models, as the range was moving toward its major revamp for 1971. This did not include the Royal Star which was dropped at the end of 1970 to leave just the three 654 cc twins with the same names but completely new cycle parts.

The engines were as before with a single carburettor for the A65T and twins for the A65L and A65FS. This last model retained its two exhaust pipes and silencers on the left at waist level as before, but with a matt black finish which contrasted with the dove grey frame colour common to all.

The frame, and most other cycle parts, were common to those used by Triumph at that time, although there were some minor differences here and there to keep owners and dealers on their toes. The main section of the frame was a large diameter tube which formed the top and seat section while also carrying the engine oil. The down and subframe tubes were duplex to form a good, rigid structure.

A rebuilt 1968 Mk IV Spitfire with twin leading shoe front brake and Amal Concentric carburettors. All need to be first in line for the crankshaft improvements now possible if they are to run at speed for long.

The front forks were slimline without gaiters so prey to stones damaging their stanchions, causing the seals to leak. The headlamp shell was carried on bent wire brackets and the speedometer and rev-counter in supports attached to the fork top. The Thunderbolt was without the second instrument, one of the few differences it had from the Lightning.

All three models had the same conical hubs for both wheels with an 8 in. twin leading shoe brake at the front and a 7 in. at the rear. The front brake cam levers were too short to work effectively, and the same hub was also used by the four-stroke singles.

The machine lines were set by the new frame, forks and hubs along with new side covers and air filter boxes. There were no covers for the rear spring units, and a hand-rail was fitted round the dualseat which was without a hump. It was also too high from the ground and shared this problem with Triumph, which made the twins awkward for riders below average height.

The company was by then in deep financial trouble but did list the two road twins for 1972, although the Firebird Scrambler was by then no more. The frames and seats were amended to lower the riding height and the frame colour returned to its traditional black.

For America the A70L Lightning was created to provide the basis for a track racing machine and was also referred to as the Lightning 75. It had the engine stroke extended to raise the capacity to 751 cc and quite a number of special engine parts including the crankcase, pistons, rods and flywheel as well as the crankshaft. A few engines stayed in England and found their way into chassis, but the 200 built as complete machines went to the United States.

By the late 1960s all the twins were built in export form, hence the small tank and high bars on this 1969 A50 Royal Star.

94

This was one of the final acts of the beleaguered company, for 1972 was their last year in the old form at the Small Heath factory. They became involved in complex financial and company moves involving the government at times, plus both Norton and Triumph. There was no real answer to these troubles for BSA and, although the name was to reappear, the firm closed and in time the Small Heath factory was demolished.

The plant did produce parts for a while and the name appeared on one more group product, this being the 1973 T65 Thunderbolt. However, for all its BSA name and tank transfer, this was simply a TR6 Triumph of that period fitted with the older twin leading shoe front brake as used in 1969–70.

Prospects

These unit twins never quite reached the level of popularity of the pre-unit twins, and somehow lacked their style and easy riding. However, they are large capacity twins and thus rate average at least as a popular and mainly reliable series with good spares supplies.

There are exceptions and problems, but these can be overcome to a good degree so the machines can offer good, classic motorcycling. The major snag lies with the crankshaft and main bearings after the drive side ball race was changed to a roller race for 1966. This removed the positive location of the crankshaft which was from then on allowed to wander between the single lip of the roller outer and the flange of the timing side bush, with shims and a thrust washer to limit the play.

This was a dreadful piece of engineering, for a roller race is just not meant to work in this way. The loads were too much for the thrust washer fitted on the timing side, and the parts soon wore to increase the clear-

This is the 1970 Lightning with home-market tank. It has gained a balance pipe for the exhaust system but is otherwise much as before.

ance. This allowed the crankshaft, no light-weight and spinning at high speed, to move about and overload the shims as well.

The problem was made worse by the lubrication system which had not changed in principle since the first A7. It began with a pump which, for the unit twins, had an alloy body prone to distortion and thus leaks and low output pressure. This fed the timing side bush which was drilled so the oil lubricated it and flowed into the crankshaft to the big end bearings. The pressure that reached the left bearing was always low because it came at the end of the line, and that of both big ends and the main also depended on the wear of the right bearing bush.

The combination of the pump, oil feed and crankshaft location are such that it is all too easy for the bush to turn in its housing. This cuts off the oil supply to the big ends and main so they seize and usually break the rods which then smash the crankcase.

This invariably happens more with the sports engines, especially when combined

The 1971 models had a new frame, forks, conical hubs and many detail parts but the seat was too high and time was running out for this Lightning.

with a high compression ratio and used on the road. The Spitfire thus has a fragile engine in its stock form, as would the Wasp and Hornet if anyone could ride them fast enough off-road. On the street they have exactly the same problem, perhaps made worse by lower gearing.

The problem is compounded by the vibration levels reached by any vertical twin, especially when 650 cc and 6500 rpm are exceeded. The unit twin therefore sits on one limit and may run over the other to be marginal. Couple this with some poor crankshaft balancing at the factory in the late 1960s and the inherently poor design and trouble is always waiting to strike.

Fortunately there are solutions to these problems, with a start being a new oil pump with a cast-iron body. These do not distort, hold their pressure and have a long working life. The next change is harder to carry out but just as essential, as it replaces the timing side bush with a combined ball and roller bearing which can positively locate the crankshaft. This allows the drive side roller race to simply carry the radial loads it was designed for, and the mains then have no trouble in doing their job.

The new timing side race cuts off the oil feed so the crankshaft has to be modified to deal with this. It is done by also altering the outer cover so the oil is fed into the end of the crankshaft on its centre line and just runs along this line and then out to the big ends. This eases the load on the pump as centrifugal force now helps the oil out to the bearings and does not, as before, work against it even entering the shaft.

Any work of this nature is likely to affect the alignment of the primary drive, another area that BSA failed to get right. They did provide a means of altering the line of the engine sprocket but undid the good work once the crankshaft was allowed to float to any degree. Alignment is important, as without it the triplex chain will wear quickly. But before attempting to align the parts the crankshaft must be positively located by the main bearing change.

There is another modification well worth carrying out in the primary chaincase which affects clutch operation. The clutch tends to be heavy as standard because there is no real location for the clutch rod to run in the centre of the pressure plate, and this plus the loads causes the trouble. The solution is a new pressure plate with radial needle race, which greatly reduces the friction between plate and thrust rod while preventing the latter from wandering off-centre. It is a cheap and successful modification well worth doing to any unit twin.

These points may all seem like good reasons for avoiding the unit twins, but this is not so due to the available remedies. It adds up to a machine with plenty of strengths and a few weaknesses that can be cured. Given these, careful assembly, proper maintenance and some degree of restraint of maximum engine speed, the BSA unit twin is a fine motorcycle.

As all but the youngest are at least twenty years old now, it makes sense not to abuse them, but 70 mph cruising should be no trouble. One carburettor is less trouble than two, while the performance difference is marginal and low-compression pistons will make for a happier engine as will good balancing and well-fitted engine bolts.

The styling is always round and egg-like, so does not appeal to as many tastes as the pre-unit models. But the combination of all factors means a minimum of three stars for any unit twin. Only the Spitfire and A70L reach the five-star level, as much for rarity as anything. The Spitfire was listed only for three years, with changes for each year, and there cannot be many left with the original engine. The 750 is simply rare and thus rather special.

BSA FIREBIRD SCRAMBLER 650

The revised 1971 range included this Firebird Scrambler with its smart exhaust system raised on the left under a mesh grill.

For the rest it is three stars for the touring A50, A65 and A65T, with four stars for the sports models mainly because they are always preferred even if the tourers are nicer to ride. The T65 earns three stars, for it is simply a touring Triumph with a badge change.

Therefore, as always, the choice depends on use. For riding, a well-sorted Thunderbolt from the late 1960s could give the best combination of virtues. For show, it is a different matter and a Lightning Clubman, Cyclone or Spitfire is more likely to be selected.

The rare A70L built for the USA but here seen in later years back in its home country. It used the stock cycle parts including the poor front brake.

★★★★★	Rocket 3 A75	1968–70
★★★★	Rocket 3 A75	1971–72
★★★★★	Rocket 3 A75V	1972

The Rocket 3

The BSA Rocket 3 was something of an anomaly, for it was designed at Meriden in the Triumph offices but built at Small Heath in the BSA factory. It was accompanied by the Triumph Trident which used the same basic engineering, shared many detail parts but had major changes in others.

The engine was the first of these changes. The BSA had the cylinders inclined forward a little, unlike the Triumph which had them set vertically. The Trident also had a typical Triumph timing cover and from the right looked similar to their unit-construction twin, but the Rocket differed from this and the BSA twins as well.

The two three-cylinder machines were conceived during the 1960s and launched in 1968 for export only, so did not reach their home market until the next year. The engine was based heavily on the Triumph twin and used much of its engineering in a rather complex and expensive manner, which arose because the prototype was made using many twin parts for convenience. BSA intended to change this for production, but once the firm decided to go ahead there was no time for any major alteration so the prototype design was used.

Triples

The 740 cc engine thus had a three-part crankcase with the two outers much as the case halves of a twin, with the centre acting as a distance piece. All three were both awkward and expensive to produce,

especially the centre piece which extended back to carry the gearbox. It was open at the top of the crankcase section and in this went the lower halves of two plain main bearings with caps which bolted down on them.

Rocket 3 in its original 1968 form with early type twin leading shoe front brake, here carrying a works tester and with the factory in the background.

Drive side of the Rocket 3 with triplex chain and diaphragm clutch under the polished cover. Engine and frame numbers A75R 125, so an early example. A very fast motorcycle.

The outer halves carried the main bearings with a ball race on the drive side and a roller on the timing side. They also had bushes for the two camshafts which ran across the engine, high up and fore and aft in Triumph fashion. Both castings extended back a little to carry the oil pump on the left and a filter on the right, with bolts and studs to hold them to the centre section.

A one-piece crankshaft ran in the four main bearings with alloy connecting rods with plain big end shells. The gudgeon pins ran directly in the rods and the three-ring pistons moved in a one-piece alloy block with pressed-in liners. There were Triumph-type tappets and guide blocks at front and back of the block, with the pushrods enclosed in tubes placed between each pair of cylinders.

The cylinder head was another one-piece alloy casting, and in Meriden-style had separate rocker boxes for each line of valves. Each box had an oil feed into one end of its long rocker spindle and a one-piece lid with

The 1969 Rocket 3 with bellcrank front brake, here lined up in front of a row of Triumphs.

Show stand under footrests and the distinctive ray gun silencers fitted on the first models.

this and the box well-finned for cooling. There were three separate inlet stubs bolted to the head with an Amal Concentric carburettor for each. These were fitted to a manifold which connected to the stubs with rubber hoses and carried a linkage, so that one cable from the twistgrip opened all three throttles.

On the exhaust side there were adaptors screwed into the ports, with a manifold clamped to all three by finned rings. The outer pipes of the manifold ran out and down to crankcase level where each was fitted to an exhaust pipe which ran back to a low-level silencer on each side. The centre pipe divided into two and then ran into the outer pipes, so the total effect was three into four into two.

The silencers were one of the special features of the machine, with a flattened oval section that tapered out along its length. At the tail each was cut off at an angle and the end plate which blanked it off carried three short outlet pipes. It was these pipes that gave them the name "ray gun" silencers, which they kept from then on.

The timing side of the engine was Triumph on the inside but BSA for the exterior. Under the cover there was a train of gears to drive the two camshafts, with the exhaust one driving the points cam via an auto-advance and the rev-counter from the shaft centre. The counter spindle went in a housing set in the front of the centre crankcase casting, and the points fired three separate coils mounted as a group.

The alternator also went under the timing cover on the right end of the crankshaft, and the duplex gear oil pump was gear driven from the left end. The lubrication system was dry sump, with an external oil tank plus a cooler which sat above the engine under the nose of the petrol tank.

A triplex primary chain took the drive to the single-plate diaphragm-spring clutch and had a pair of slipper tensioners. The clutch ran dry in its own cast chamber which was positioned behind the left outer crank-

The drive side of the 1970 Rocket 3 retained the original lines and was little altered. The brakes were marginal for such a fast and heavy machine.

case. In this way the inner primary chaincase could bolt to both parts and form the outer wall of the clutch chamber. The clutch sprocket was thus in the chaincase and had a shock absorber built into its centre, with this splined to the clutch input shaft.

The clutch lift mechanism went into the outer primary chaincase under its own small cover, with a ball and ramp design and the cable run into the top of the casting. This also carried a needle race for the clutch sprocket centre, so this was adequately supported on both sides against the chain's pull.

The gearbox was a stock Triumph with four speeds right down to the change mechanism and kickstart. The inner and outer

The 1971 Rocket 3 with small tank, slimline forks and new group conical wheel hubs. The front had a twin leading shoe brake but the cam levers were too short to be effective.

covers did differ so that the latter blended into one, with the timing cover and the gear pedal was shaped to suit.

The engine unit went into a frame much as that used by the twins of that period and totally unlike the Triumph with its bolted-on subframe. It was thus a fully welded cradle frame with single top tube and duplex downtubes, which swept under the engine unit and up to form the subframe.

The forks and wheels were stock group parts common to both marques and also used by the twins. Fork gaiters protected the stanchions and the top shrouds supported the separate headlamp shell. The front hub had the full-width cast-iron brake drum, and the brake itself was twin leading shoe with the cable sweeping in from the rear. At the rear went an offset hub with single leading shoe brake. Both wheels had 19 in. rims.

The oil tank went under the front of the dualseat on the right, with the battery beside it and the tools behind that. Large side covers carrying the Rocket 3 legend enclosed this area, and their style was continued in the large petrol tank and its combined knee-grips and badges. Beneath it there was styl-ing trim for the oil cooler and a one-piece box for the air filter supplying the three carburettors.

It all added up to a large and impressive motorcycle finished generally in black with the petrol tank, mudguards and side covers in red or lime green. On the road its performance proved up to expectations with a top speed in excess of 120 mph and acceleration to match. Handling was good, the machine was comfortable to ride and it made the right type of noise—always an important point with a motorcycle.

Less desirable was its healthy thirst for petrol, and when the performance was used its marginal brakes were hard pressed to slow the relatively heavy machine. There were also various troubles with the early machines which indicated once more the folly of going into production before development was complete and all lessons incorporated.

It was also bad luck, or poor timing, that saw the Rocket 3 appear at the same time as the first Honda CB750 which promptly upstaged it. The Japanese machine offered four cylinders, overhead camshaft, five

Final year for the Rocket 3 was 1972 when the seat hump went and the frame colour returned to the usual black. Right at the end there was a five-speed option.

speeds, electric start and a front disk brake on a mass-produced motorcycle sold worldwide. This had never happened before.

The BSA triple sold but at a fairly slow rate compared with the Trident, and early in 1969 came onto its home market. By then it had the bellcrank lever for the front brake and continued for 1970 with a number of minor changes. One was to lower the gearing a little which made the machine more flexible on the road.

The Rocket 3 underwent alterations to its cycle parts for 1971 as part of the range revamp that cost BSA so dearly. The engine unit and frame were little altered, but megaphone silencers were fitted and the front forks changed to the group slimline type without gaiters but with bent wire headlamp supports. Both wheels changed to the conical hubs and the front contained the twin leading shoe brake with too-short cam levers common to many other models.

The mudguards became chrome-plated sports blades and the oil cooler lost its end covers while the standard petrol tank was a small 2½ gallon type from the older twins with pear-shaped badges. Fortunately the four-gallon tank used up to then was retained for the home market and this capacity was essential in view of the engine's thirst.

As with the other models that year, the frame of the triple was finished in dove grey while the petrol tank and side covers alone were in flamboyant red for the home market. The small tank was finished in grey with chrome side panels, and the side covers matched this in the grey.

The gearing was again lowered for 1972 when the dualseat lost its hump, but the main change was to the finish. The frame went back to black, the front brake backplate became matt black and the tank and upper side cover were in burgundy. The big petrol tank became standard with the small one an

The Craig Vetter styling for the triple was normally used by the Triumph Hurricane but is here seen with BSA on the tank—appropriate as the machine used the BSA engine and frame.

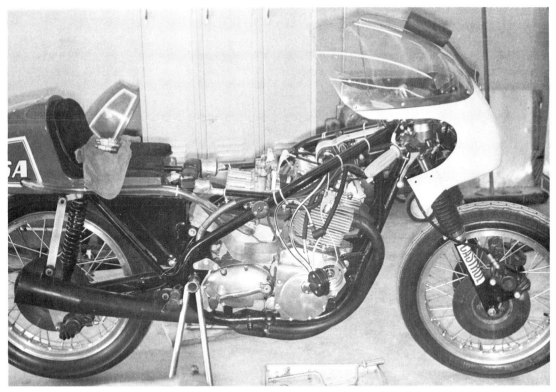

The racing works triple at Daytona in 1972. These machines carried both BSA and Triumph labels indiscriminately and could vary from meeting to meeting. The howl of the exhaust is still remembered and much missed.

option. Late in the day came one further option: this was a five-speed gearbox, which also went in the Trident, and in this form the Rocket 3 became the A75V.

Sadly, that was the end of its line. BSA failed as a company, although the triple engine continued to be built at Small Heath into 1974. The Trident adopted the BSA engine form with its inclined block for 1975–76, and the same unit was also used for its stylish X75 Hurricane of 1973. But that was after the last Rocket 3 had been built.

Prospects

Five stars for the early triple models built up to 1970, for the triple is a classic motorcycle that offers a fine ride as well. The 1971–72 machines with the revised forks and wheels are down to four stars, although still desirable and possibly will move up to five anyway. Five stars plus for a genuine five-speed machine, as there cannot have been many built. But beware of conversions.

In fact, be wary on all counts. First, check on the dating aspect to make sure the machine on offer has not had a later Triumph engine fitted to it. This is not a problem in itself, as long as the fact is known, acknowledged and allowed for. Second is the machine itself. While the engine is a strong one, it must be well-assembled, properly set up and correctly maintained to give its best.

If this is not done the performance will soon drop off and problems will arise. Sorted out you will be riding one of the truly great motorcycles.

Chapter 9

War and prototypes

★★★	M20	1939–45
★★★★	M20 plus ohv	1945
★★	C10	WD
★★/★★★	C11	WD
★★★★	WB30	1941
★★★★	WD twin	1944
★★	B40M	1967
★★	B40RR	1969
★★★★	Side-valve twin	1951
★★★★★	MC1 250 cc	1954
★★★	Beeza	1955
★★★★	Fury	1971

During World War II, records show that BSA supplied 126,334 motorcycles to the armed services, along with vast quantities of other material which naturally included

Wartime M20 as refurbished in later years, complete with service number and other insignia on the khaki paint. Side valves and simple but sturdy construction.

many guns and rifles. Most of the motorcycles were the prosaic M20 model but there were others, including prototypes.

In the years after the war BSA had less to do with the military field but did supply some unit singles in the late 1960s. Some of the older B range singles were sold to European forces in the late 1940s but the firm did not play a major role in the postwar military marketplace, for it was busy enough with its standard range of machines.

Prototype BSA models rarely came out of the factory. Failures were invariably buried in the famous BSA "hole in the ground" while the more successful would be developed on for production. Thus not many of the interesting reminders of what might have been have survived but there are a few, some good and some less so.

Military machines

The bulk of military machines were the M20 and they were little altered from the civilian model listed for 1940. Certain home comforts such as footrest rubbers were soon dispensed with, but the basic machine was the same.

This meant a perfectly standard engine. The few changes that were made applied to its external accessories rather than the main assembly. One was an immobiliser, for it became illegal from July 1940 to leave a machine unattended without locking a wheel or removing a part to prevent it working. An accepted method was to have a join in the high-tension lead so that part could be removed to leave the remainder too short, and BSA did this.

The carburettor was changed to a design with internal air passages but kept to its former size. The alteration sealed off four air bleed holes so that all the air had to flow through the main intake and could thus be filtered. No air cleaner was fitted as standard, but for desert use one was mounted on top of the petrol tank where it was held by straps. It was connected to the carburettor by rubber hose and to allow this the right rear corner of the tank was cut away.

At the other end of the engine cycle the silencer was tilted up a trifle to raise its outlet. The rest of the machine was stock M20 with a few alterations and additions. An undershield was fitted to protect the engine, and there was no instrument panel in the tank top. In place of this the speedometer went on the top of the girder forks and the ammeter and light switch in a small panel in the back of the headlamp. The switch had a position to turn on the taillight only, as well as the usual off, side and headlights, as this was needed for convoy duties.

There was a mask on the headlamp to keep its output down and out of sight of aircraft.

A rear carrier and pannier frames with canvas bags were fitted and a small pillion seat could be added but seldom was. A hefty prop stand was provided in the form of a

Posed picture of an M20 in use during the dark days of 1940. Don R's played their part using machines such as the BSA, which were sold off postwar with a change of colour.

The BSA WB30 which was derived from the prewar B29. A much better machine for the services, it was never to go into production until postwar as the B31 series.

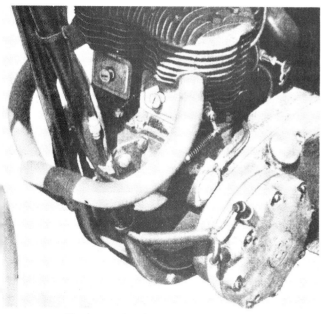

Engine unit of the wartime BSA twin with its rear-mounted carburettor feeding through the iron block to the front side valves. Early type alternator provided current.

spike with a guard to give support in mud, and the rider was issued a handbook and a comprehensive toolkit for daily servicing tasks.

The M20 was a heavy, clumsy motorcycle for service use which had to contend with normal highway use and muddy tracks near the battle zone. BSA was well aware of this and in response produced the WB30 in 1941, based on the B29 the firm had introduced for the 1940 range and from which the postwar B31 was to come.

For the wartime single the B29 base had the right combination of parts with the strong M range bottom half and lighter top end. The new engine had hairpin valve springs so the chambers in the one-piece head and rocker box were much larger than those of the B31, but otherwise the two engines were really the same.

The main change was to the generator; while ignition continued to be supplied by a magneto, this had an alternator strapped to its back. This supplied direct lighting to the headlamp, much as on a two-stroke, while

Military B40M of 1967, which was based on a combination of the B40E and C15T models, both no longer in the lists by then, but whose features combined to produce what the services needed.

there was a dry battery for parking and a bulb horn.

The transmission and cycle parts came mainly from the prewar B range and included rather small brakes. This was just one of the measures carried out to keep the weight down which came out at something like eighty pounds less than an M20. With a more responsive engine the result was a much livelier machine that could power through mud and be easily lifted over rocks and steps with a quick flick of the throttle wrist. A desirable trail machine, really.

The prototype was shown off carrying the BSA350 registration number used postwar by one of the works trials machines. Later, it or another went on the roads as FOM719 and was given a service number C4379578 while the War Office ran it through a series of tests. They liked what they found so issued a contract for a small number of machines, possibly fifty, to be built and tested by the army.

Naturally the army was delighted with the new machine after coping with the M20, and an order for a batch of 10,000 was placed with BSA. Sadly for the Don R's, this was later amended to M20s, to avoid spares complications it was said, so there were no more WB30 machines built.

An offshoot of the M20, which were abandoned in great number all over Europe after the war, was an early postwar conversion kit. This was made by La Mototecnica Velox of Turin which produced similar kits for Italian side-valve engine. All were designed to convert the motors to overhead valves. For the M20 it comprised an alloy head and barrel with the pushrod tunnel integral with each part. With these went a suitable piston and other detail items that included odd, hairpin valve springs which each worked on both valves. The appearance of the conversion was not unlike a B31 but without the pushrod tunnel, and the converted machine would do about 70 mph.

While the M20 provided the bulk of the wartime military BSA machines, and the WB30 the interest, the firm also built some smaller models for training use. These were based on the 249 cc C10, and while this was adequate for its normal job it found army life rather hard to take. The combination of trainee use plus long hours of home duties gave rise to various shortcomings, but the machines were cheap so served their purpose.

There was also a batch of C11 machines built for service in India and for this they were fitted with a mag-dyno in place of the usual coil ignition. In other respects both lightweights were as the prewar models, but in a khaki finish and with service fitments.

Toward the end of the war the Ministry of Supply issued a specification for a replacement army machine which called for a 500 cc twin-cylinder four-stroke engine to meet the parameters. These covered speed, weight, consumption, water fording, noise and hill climbing along with various details. Triumph, BSA and Douglas all offered prototypes in due course.

The BSA had its roots in a wartime exercise around 1944 and its engine was a 500 cc vertical twin with its side valves at the front. The camshaft thus ran across the front of the crankcase, unlike the A7 twin, but much else was as for the civilian model including the rear-mounted gear-driven magneto. The Solex carburettor went at the rear of the one-piece cast-iron block which had a tortuous path cast through it to form the inlet tract. The two exhaust ports splayed out from the block corners, and the cylinder head was a one-piece alloy casting.

The three-speed gearbox was bolted to the rear of the crankcase and had footchange. The primary chain that drove it was enclosed in a cast alloy case and this carried an alternator which attached to the outer. It supplied the headlamp directly, but it was later intended to add a rectifier and battery.

The rear chain was also fully enclosed with an alloy casting and ran at fixed centres, for the rear wheel had no fore or aft adjustment. Instead, there was a jockey sprocket on an eccentric mounting in the case and this set the chain tension.

The engine unit went into a rigid frame with duplex downtubes, and this was fitted with telescopic front forks. The wheels had 19 in. rims and 7 in. brakes in offset hubs so were stock BSA, but the tank was not; both the speedometer and toolbox were set in its top. The saddle had adjustments for both height and position along the machine while the usual service panniers were fitted, plus a pillion seat.

The machine was ridden in the 1948 Scottish Six Days Trial and gained an award but was not taken any further. At that time the army had far more machines than it needed, despite selling off large batches for a transport-hungry public, so had no call for new ones. The Triumph twin was to fare a little better, but that sold much more for export for some years, so BSA really did the best thing in concentrating on their civilian market. After all, they bought Triumph in 1951, so the business simply came into the group by another door.

It was a long time before BSA built another machine for the army, well into the 1960s in fact. This was the B40M Military model of 1967 which was based heavily on the B40E Enduro and late C15T machines. It had the B40 engine with its low compression ratio but a wide-ratio gearbox with ratios not used by other models. The carburettor was usually a special Amal with butterfly throttle and a massive air filter, but a Concentric type was also listed and used by some machines.

The oil system was improved by fitting a cartridge-type filter in the return line, and the engine unit went into the competition frame with minor changes. It had a pivoted rear fork and telescopics with gaiters at the front while the wheels were in the older style. Thus the front had a screw-in spindle and offset hub and the rear the crinkle hub and quickly detachable facility.

At first a 20 in. front rim was specified along with an 18 in. rear, but this also changed in time so both wheels had the same 18 in. size. Off-road tyres were fitted to them, and other areas altered during production were the exhaust system and seat. The first could be tucked in as on the trials model or low down as for the road, while the second could be a single or dual. In either case the competition-type oil tank was used and a full rear chaincase fitted.

The Military model was also built as the B40 Rough Rider in 1969, but this was effectively the same machine although both had

their own parts list. The later machine ran on from the first so had the 18 in. wheels and Concentric carburettor in all cases.

Prospects

The collection of militaria is a major hobby that touches on motorcycles in only a small way. Thus, there is a group of people who have a foot in both camps, and this affects the rating and value of the models. To fetch the best returns the machine needs to be in its service clothes and to have, if possible, some indication of its military history.

This pushes the rating of an ex-military M20 up to three stars as long as it is in full military trim. This should include the carrier and panniers as well as the khaki finish, army number and regimental insignia. If the M20 has the Italian ohv conversion then it

British Army motorcycle 250

The BSA version of the Canadian Bombardier with Austrian Rotax engine unit as assembled in the British plant in 1979 with a number of UK sourced components.

rises to four stars, for it would be a rare machine and an interesting one to own.

The WB30 and prototype military twin also rate four stars as both are rare and important steps in BSA history. The rest, that is the two 250s and twin B40 models, earn only two stars. The C11 could rise to three on the basis of being rare, but not the C10. The B40s, on the other hand, could sink a touch unless in absolutely original condition.

Prototypes

Not many prototypes are on the market, as BSA preferred to bury its mistakes and develop the successes. Four are worth mentioning, though: the Beeza scooter, the racing MC1, a prototype side-valve twin and the Fury twin.

The first has already been described in chapter two, while the second showed the depth of expertise and fresh thinking that existed in the BSA concern, often unused by the top brass. The MC1 was a road racing

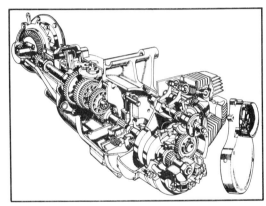

Side-valve engine unit and in-line transmission of the Beezer scooter which hung from a single pivot point and was controlled by one suspension leg.

machine built with the aim of developing a strong design that could then be detuned for road use in sports or touring forms.

The engine was a single of 248 cc with a near horizontal cylinder. It had four valves

The Beezer scooter, with its rather Germanic lines, lacked the chic style of the Italians and their light and airy looks. The side-valve engine did not promise much performance.

arranged in a radial layout with these opened by two single overhead camshafts and rockers. There were two shafts as each lay at an angle across the head to match the valves, and one drove the other by shallow-angle bevels. The drive up to them was also by bevels with a vertical shaft, so there were three pairs in all, but couplings in the shafts eased the task of meshing the bevels.

The vertical shaft was driven directly from the crankshaft which was a one-piece forging with split connecting rod and plain big end bearing. An outside flywheel went on the left and cooling was by air with ample finning on the main components and the minor covers.

Ignition was at first by magneto and later by coil, and there were two carburettors on parallel inlet ports. For the exhaust, a pipe ran low down on each side to a shallow taper megaphone with small reverse cone. The primary chain ran in a well-finned case on the left to drive a four-speed gearbox via a dry clutch run outside the case in the air.

The frame and forks were equally unusual with the first of duplex loop form, with the tube pairs crossing over just behind the headstock. At the rear went a pivoted rear fork controlled by a single spring and damper unit mounted up under the seat and connected to a triangulated part of the rear fork.

The front forks were of the Earles leading link type, with the main part built up from pressings. The whole assembly pivoted on head races as usual, but less usual was the location of the outer race in the fork while the inner fitted to a stem clamped into the frame as the headstock.

An oil tank went under the seat and the machine was usually seen with a crude, ugly but purposeful petrol tank. Both wheels had single leading shoe brakes with the front one floating in a full-width hub. Alloy rims and racing tyres were fitted but no fairing.

On test the machine proved encouraging and was tried by Geoff Duke at Oulton Park where he lapped quickly enough to highlight the need for better brakes and a five-speed

The BSA 250 cc road racing MC1 had great potential but was brought to nought by a weak BSA boardroom. The four-valve head, unusual steering head and monoshock rear suspension all show the depth of advanced thought the design office could produce.

gearbox. Even without those improvements, Duke was enthusiastic enough to enter the machine for a Silverstone race, but at the last moment the BSA board called it off. Thus the 32 bhp BSA did not run in the race which was won by a 28 bhp NSU ridden by John Surtees.

So the MC1 was put away and not seen again for a long time, but it still exists.

The side-valve twin engine was built in the early 1950s and then lost for some thirty-five years before it surfaced again. It was designed by Bert Hopwood to power a military machine, and he also foresaw it being used as a utility motorcycle with enclosing pressed-steel chassis.

The engine had the same bore and stroke as the A7 so its capacity was 497 cc, and the two parallel cylinders were inclined well forward. All the main castings were in light alloy with each half of the vertically split crankcase including one cylinder. This had an iron liner and its own cylinder head, so only the inlet manifold joined the two sides above the crankcase mouth.

The side valves lay at an angle to the bore, much as in the Beeza scooter engine, and were opened by tappets with adjusters. There were bronze guides for the valves, inserts for the valve seats and bushes for the tappets, with an access cover for setting the valve gaps. The camshaft ran in bushes in the crankcase and was driven by a train of gears on the right. The top one also drove a duplex gear oil pump for the dry-sump lubrication system, and the rest of the timing chest was filled with an alternator. This was fitted to the end of the crankshaft which was much as that of the A7 but heavier and stronger.

Ignition was by coil with the points and distributor housing located behind the engine and driven by a skew gear from the camshaft. The original carburettor was a Solex, but an Amal was used for the restoration and attached to a manifold made to fit. All the valves were at the rear of the engine which suited the carburettor but meant that the exhausts emerged from each side. The pipes thus had to turn sharply down and in before they ran back to a period silencer on each side.

The crankcase was cast with a mounting face to the rear to accept the standard semi-unit gearbox then in use on the twins. The primary drive was thus all-stock, with duplex chain and polished alloy chaincase as used before the advent of the pivoted fork frame.

This interesting engine unit was installed in an early rigid A7 frame in 1988, and fitted with cycle parts mainly from the first of the vertical twin line. The frame had to be modified a little to accept the engine, as the cylinder heads lay between the downtubes

The 497 cc all-alloy side-valve twin engine built in the early 1950s with a view of military or utility use but never to come to anything.

The side-valve twin engine in the set of cycle parts found for it in 1988 to show off the experimental unit. A fine example of marque enthusiasm.

and also fastened to them with a head steady. The forks were from the 1946–48 period and the machine was finished off with a period petrol tank decorated by chrome plating, with top and side panels in maroon with gold lining.

The twin ran smoothly and the combination of the heavy crankshaft and side valves restricted the performance but ensured that what there was, came without fuss or trauma. Although the machine as built up was never produced by BSA, even as a prototype, it represents a fine way of showing off this experimental engine. The one that BSA

did make was for the services and had an all-welded lightweight tubular frame. It fared quite well on test but the matter was never taken further by the company.

The Fury twin was a horse of a different colour, because it was developed through to production but never went on sale. It was part of the last major group launch held late in 1970 for both BSA and Triumph machines, and was duplicated by the Triumph Bandit in the best traditions of badge engineering.

The machines were really Triumph; the original design was by Edward Turner and a prototype of this was built. It had an all-alloy

BSA FURY 350

The BSA Fury with its 350 cc twin-cylinder engine and five-speed gearbox in unit construc- tion, mounted in a duplex frame with the group slimline forks and conical hubs of 1971.

engine with inclined cylinders and gear-driven, twin overhead camshafts. Internally it had a 180 degree crankshaft which meant two carburettors and separate exhaust systems, while coil ignition and twelve-volt electrics were specified along with a four-speed gearbox driven by a duplex primary chain.

This unit-construction engine went into a light frame with pivoted fork rear suspension and forks with external springs. The wheels had 17 in. rims and the front a disk brake with mechanical operation, while the rear remained a drum. The complete machine was quick and light but lacked rigidity

Fury twin engine with the tunnel for the chain drive up to the two overhead camshafts, of which the exhaust carried the points cam.

BSA FURY 350 SS

The 350 twin was also available as the Fury SS model, built as a street scrambler. It differed in having the exhausts at waist level on the right and finished in black.

in the frame and forks so the handling was poor. In addition, the crankshaft broke too easily and the front brake tended to seize.

Before the machine was announced to press and public it was given a major revamp and about all that was kept was the 350 cc capacity, 180 degree crankshaft, inclined cylinders and twin camshafts. Most everything else was altered in one way or another, with the camshafts for one driven by chain from a shaft which was geared to the crankshaft. The chain ran on the left side of the engine within chambers cast in the head and block.

Inside the engine went a forged crankshaft, with integral central flywheel, which ran in a drive side ball and timing side roller race. Shell big ends were used with alloy rods and steel caps, while the gudgeon pins ran directly in the rods to hold three-ring pistons. These moved in iron liners pressed into the alloy block, and the head was also in alloy and incorporated the camshaft bearings. The points went on the right end of the exhaust camshaft, which cannot have helped to keep the timing constant and correct.

Lubrication was dry sump with the pump driven from the left end of the crankshaft while the alternator went on the right. Just

inboard of it went the chain drive from the optional electric starter mounted on top of the crankcase behind the block, and inboard of that went the duplex primary chain. This drove a five-speed gearbox in unit with the engine, and both pedals went on the left.

The engine was supplied with fuel by a pair of Amal Concentric carburettors and there was a choice of exhaust systems. For road use a pipe on each side ran down to a low-mounted silencer, but the street scrambler version had both systems at waist level on the right, finished in matt black and with a protective grille fitted to them.

The frame for this engine unit was duplex with a single top tube and fitted with the group slimline forks and wheels with conical hubs. The front had the 8 in. twin leading shoe brake and the rear, the 7 in., while both were spoked to 18 in. rims. The detail fittings were as used by the other models of that launch and the finish a metallic paint listed as Plum Crazy.

A few of these machines were built and reports suggest that they were quick but noisy. Handling was good as the bulk of the cycle parts were stout enough to cope with the triple, but the front brake was again only just adequate. The matter soon became academic as the twin became one of the casualties of the firm's financial troubles and so never went into production.

Prospects

High marks for any of the prototypes for interest and rarity, with the MC1 rated five stars and the side-valve and Fury twins four. The Beeza, even if it still exists, is unlikely to raise more than three, since it is a scooter and there is limited interest in these.

Except for the Fury, the machines were one-offs so will seldom change hands as is the way with such models. Even when they do they will not be advertised, for each is sure to have someone who has asked for first refusal. This may apply to the Fury as well; the small number that exist are each likely to have a customer ready to purchase if given the opportunity.

Few Fury machines ever left the factory but this is one of them. It shows off the light grey frame finish which few riders liked.

Chapter 10

Looking and buying

The previous chapters have sought to tell you about the different BSA ranges and models so you know how they fit together, their extent and how they came and went. You now need to plan how to find what you seek, how to look it over and how to negotiate an acceptable price.

The BSA make was one of the most popular of the postwar era, and the machines have continued in this role in the classic re-

One for a restorer and not the machine to buy unless you want that type of project. If you do, then this is mostly all there and has a useful pair of alloy rims. It needs a full rebuild.

vival of the 1980s. The marque exists in large numbers and Bantams, singles and twins are all equally easy to find in a variety of forms and specifications. The choice will not be so large if you are seeking one of the more glamorous models, such as the Gold Star or Rocket 3, but they are about and can be found although this may not be easy.

This situation is both helped and hindered by the way in which many of the parts will interchange across many models, which can bring problems as well. Be extra careful where this can be done, such as with the pivoted fork frames and all their cycle parts, for there are a good number of pre-unit twins about which actually have a B31 frame complete with its oil pump kink in the right rail.

This may have come about for good reasons, but is more likely to be the result of an autojumble special in which case there may be little that matches at all. Note too that any Bantam engine will fit any Bantam frame, although the electrics could be more trouble to fix up correctly. Check any claim that the engine has been swopped to produce a learner legal (in the United Kingdom) machine of 125 cc, as it could just as easily be a 150.

All Gold Star engines have an engine prefix that begins with the series type, such as ZB or DBD, followed by 32 for the smaller and 34 for the larger and then the essential GS before the serial number. Remember that the alloy B series engine can look just like a Gold Star but is not. Be equally careful about the Rocket Gold Star, whose frame number has a GA10 prefix and not the usual A7 one used by the rest of the twins. And do not forget that the Super Flash is just the same except that its prefix is BA10.

The C10 in its final 1953 year when the tank badge and style was altered to jazz up what is really a prosaic model; the older finish sat better.

One of the tasks of this book is to help solve these problems by providing the buyer with the information he or she needs when viewing a prospect. However, don't forget that the seller too may have a copy, so always be on your guard.

Buying any motorcycle is a process of location, viewing and negotiation, best done in that order. At all stages, the more you know the better the situation will be regardless of what you are buying or where from. A crisp remark that some feature cannot be original can work wonders for your self-confidence, but only if you have the data to back it up if your bluff should be called.

Tact with the remark may also help, for some owners will not take kindly to any suggestion that their masterpiece could have feet of clay. Thus, the owner's temperament should be gauged first while asking about the machine's history or you could find yourself in the street. With the more desirable models, some owners definitely will just not sell to other than what they see as a good home for their machine, and set themselves up as judge and jury on this. As demand usually exceeds supply there is no way round this if you want the machine, but invariably the owner will respond to your enthusiasm.

Determining your needs

Before you try to locate your BSA, you should first decide which model you want and what you will use it for. Sounds obvious, but all too often a machine is bought on impulse and within weeks is found not to fit the new owner's needs, wishes or pocket. It's much better to think it out first, even though many of the factors may conflict and chance can always play its role to place the unexpected in your hands.

One of the many unit singles in the form of the 1961 SS80 with highly tuned and rather fragile engine, which is happier if given a lower compression ratio.

Your needs, if you intend to ride the machine on a daily basis, are a good deal different than those that apply if you wish to exhibit at shows. Between these two extremes are weekend use, regular rallies or occasional rides, and all place varying demands on the machine.

Anything approaching regular use suggests that you will need to sacrifice originality for better brakes, lights, tyres and suspension. All can be altered without losing the BSA lines, and for many owners this gives them a most desirable result. They finish up with the marque they want but updated and amended to use modern technology to keep pace with modern traffic. This is a philosophy from the postwar era, when it was a common practice for machines to be modified to improve them, update them or simply adapt them better to their owner's need.

For regular riding it may be necessary to carry out some internal improvements as well to make the mechanical parts more reliable. The late twin engine timing side main is one such area, as is the oil pump on some engines and the electrics on many Bantams.

To the restorer and concours exhibitor, original fitments are everything. With the rapid growth of the classic movement this

Rebuilt side-valve single with nice right-side box sidecar finished in a Continental livery.

Meets the call for complete, correct and condition without any trouble.

has brought its own set of problems, for some parts that turn up are new-old-stock (NOS) and thus genuine even if ancient. Others are reproduction parts and their quality can vary greatly. If they are internal parts they may affect reliability, while if external they may alter the appearance. Carburettors, exhaust systems, tank rubbers, footrest rubbers, transfers and tyres are all items that wear or deteriorate so are likely to need replacement. Somehow, to the experienced eye, reproduction parts always look to be that, even in a photograph.

Your intended use will indicate the model and era that you should seek, but this is always subject to what you can afford. For many of us this may mean an adjustment and we have to settle for a Bantam or a C15 rather than the Gold Star or Rocket 3 we crave. Once you have gotten over the initial disappointment, it's much better to own a machine you really can afford than one that is stretching your resources to breaking point.

The amount you spend on the machine is never the end, either. There are always further costs with any motorcycle. How much depends on the condition when you bought it and how much you wish to do to it. A no-expense-spared restoration job can run into a large sum if you farm the work out, and a sizable one even when you do much of the work yourself. Do not take on more than your workshop or abilities can cope with, and do not delude yourself on this

Worth a look for a restorer as it has most of the major parts and would not take too much to turn into a pristine and valuable CB34 Gold Star.

Nice middle-of-the-road twin from 1966, a Royal Star or Thunderbolt. Both are nice to use on a regular basis without the hassle of twin carbs.

point. If you *do,* you can easily pull the machine apart and get stuck, then find you cannot afford the services of a specialist and have to dispose of the resultant basket job at a loss. Set your sights at an attainable level and accept that you may not have the facilities or skills to do it all. Few of us have.

All this must be taken into account and you should plan to leave yourself enough money after the purchase to cover tax, insurance and any needed work. The last item will nearly always come to twice your estimate.

Gaining knowledge

Before you start hunting for your machine, find out as much about it as you can. You are holding a good deal of what you need in your hand right now, so read it before you go shopping, not afterwards. That way you can be more certain of getting what will be the best buy for you. It is impor-

tant that you keep that last line in mind, and buy for *your* needs and not someone else's. Ignore them and concentrate on you, for if you are happy with your machine, it is of no account what others may think of your choice.

Add to your knowledge by checking prices for both private and dealer machines, with notes on the machine condition. As you will soon learn, they come in many forms ranging from the bare bones at an autojumble up to a concours restoration job bought from a specialist dealer. Machines may be original or not, complete or not, shabby, rusty or partly restored. They can be badly restored, which may be worse since a poor exterior job can indicate untold horrors under the covers.

Build up your store of knowledge so you can begin to make a reasonably accurate assessment of most models and conditions. That way, you should buy at the right price

The 1963 trials C15T with tucked-in exhaust system but still with dreadful energy transfer ignition, which must be changed for anything that will be better.

unless you let your heart rule your head. Fight this, if you can, so you at least keep to a sensible price if not the best one.

Locating the machine

The possible sources for finding the right machine are dealers, small advertisements in local papers and specialised magazines, auctions, local and one-make clubs, autojumbles and personal contacts. All need to be followed up, especially if you are after a rare model. Machines such as the early Star Twin seldom come onto the market, for most already have a queue of potential buyers who have asked the owner for first refusal.

The expensive solution is a dealer who specialises either in BSAs or vintage and classic machines. These days you are not likely to find a machine at a general bike shop at anything less than the going rate, and often it will be higher than usual because the dealer has vaguely heard that all such machines are now worth real money.

Small advertisements present two problems. One is that the worthwhile ones always seem to be a long distance away. The other problem is establishing the real condition before you set out on the journey. All too often the owner's glowing description is a bit exaggerated and the machine turns out to be too rusty, too incomplete or too poorly restored to make it a good proposition.

Even if you have travelled all day, the golden rule is to keep your money in your pocket unless you really are happy with what is on offer. We have all done the other thing more than once, but invariably pangs of regret will set in halfway back home or soon after the mistake is installed in your garage.

In this circumstance it may be worth making a silly offer. Before you open your mouth, first make two positive decisions. One is to ask yourself if you want the machine at all, even if it was free. Do not kid yourself that it will be handy for spares, because it won't. All the parts you are likely to need because your main machine is in trouble will also be worn out, split or otherwise useless. It is possible that the offering may have parts on it that you are short of or need to replace, but only allow for the price

Engine unit of the Rocket 3 had inclined cylinders and different timing and gearbox covers compared with the similar Triumph Trident.

Bevy of Easy-Rider mopeds and a Beaver. The two-speed moped worked quite well but not the single-speed one whose performance was not up to its contemporaries.

The A10 as built for the USA in 1957 with raised bars and a handrail around the dualseat. Last year for the headlamp cowl and the alloy hubs as both changed for the next.

of those parts and nothing else. Remember, they are bound to need some repair and maybe reconditioning.

Avoid machines such as this even as a present. So much is wrong that a full rebuild is needed and this could cost more than the result would be worth.

The second decision is the amount at which to pitch your silly offer. Decide on two figures, with the first your offer and the second the one you will actually go to on barter. If the owner says no way to either figure, just drive home and start hunting again.

Auctions can offer a wide selection of machines and conditions. You can look, read the description in the catalogue but not run the engine. Check carefully that the machine corresponds to its description and really is what you seek, as there is no going back. Listen to the auctioneer at the start to establish sales conditions and if there is a buyer's premium. Decide on your limit before the auction starts, write it in the catalogue and stick to it regardless. If the machine fails to reach its reserve, seek out the owner to see if you can strike a deal. After all, he or she will not have to pay commission and can hardly wish to trail the model back home again.

The local club is unlikely to provide much of a selection of machines but could give you a bargain if one happens to be what you are after. Make sure both you and the seller will be happy to meet up at the club afterwards, for a sharp deal could cost you more in the long run.

The one-make club may be a better bet, for there will be more on offer with the chance of finding some nice machines at the right price and with a decent history behind them. The BSA club in the United Kingdom produce their own magazine entitled *The Star*, and this can be a good source of machines and parts as can others produced overseas.

Autojumbles and swop meets can be a source of complete machines, but be extra careful since there is no comeback. Most machines on offer are tired and well worn, often with a fair number of items missing. Some will have engines that do not match their frames and internals not belonging to their externals. Occasionally you will find a machine that is original, is essentially complete and worth considering. The stall holder will know what it is worth so there will not be much room for bargaining, but always make the attempt.

Most purchases at autojumbles are parts or assemblies but even these need some careful checking. Check the details, and then check and check again; someday you may find a swan under the rust and grime—but not often. More likely it will say RGS on the cases but will be a Golden Flash within.

Personal contacts can be best of all. In some cases they may be your only lead to finding the rare models, so the more you have, the better your chances. While perseverance is fine, always remember to keep to the right side of the fine line between keeping in contact and becoming a nuisance and a bore.

Even trickier is the situation where the owner, usually a man, dies to leave a widow with the desirable machine. It is hardly proper etiquette to make your bid at the graveside but fatal to wait too long or another will succeed in your place. The matter of price can also be awkward, for the widow may not know or care as to the machine's value. Often a son, close relative or friend will take charge of the disposal of

A very unlikely find. The Beezer scooter on show at Earls Court late in 1955 and about the only time it was seen despite its good points of shaft drive and electric start.

the machine and other relevant items, and this at least makes it easier to conduct business.

Basket cases

Basket cases are best left alone unless you know a great deal about BSAs in which case the warning is superfluous. In theory, the various boxes shown to you contain one complete motorcycle dismantled into its component parts. In practice, the machine may have been incomplete even when the parts were together.

It is far more likely that the parts come from more than one model, often other marques as well, and will never make a complete machine. There are exceptions, but they do not occur often and the trick is to recognise one when it comes. It is also usual for the parts to be well worn, and often the result of a clearing out of a garage or workshop where the owner has had a series of similar models, and what is on offer are the discards.

Basket cases can better be viewed as a box of spares that may be useful and must be priced accordingly. Even where the seller is quite genuine about the machine and its history, it is all too easy to forget items that were missing or broken or lent to a friend. Keep well clear unless you are certain or have an expert to advise and assist you with the deal and the assembly.

Viewing the model

Some people have this down to a fine art and, with a few well-chosen phrases, imply that they are doing the seller a favour to remove the machine and really ought to be paid for this kindness. Most of us find the

going harder, but with any classic it is an essential stage.

The job depends greatly on the condition of the machine in the general sense, as this sets the standards to be looked for. A machine with rounded nuts, dull paintwork, dangling cables and an unkempt air is unlikely to be mechanically perfect inside so should be judged on that basis. A decent exterior usually implies that the interior is similar and also that it is correct for the model. Even where the outside has been spruced up in an attempt to mask an indifferent condition, it is usually fairly easy to spot this with a little practice. There will be too much polish on the main covers, none in the recesses and not enough correct settings and adjustments.

The parameters to use when viewing depend much on the use to which you will put the machine, as has been discussed already. Do not forget these or you could finish up with the wrong machine for you or the wrong price. However, whether the

Looks nice but beware if you want originality. The front mudguard and forks are from 1953, head and barrel from 1954, the tank badge too high and the silencer wrong; query the 1952 date.

machine is for daily riding or weekend showing, the state of the factors of completeness, correctness and condition all count. The degree to which they count will vary according to use, but in all cases a nice machine is worth having and a wreck is always a wreck.

There are basic inspection checks to be made when looking any machine over with a view to buy, and these apply regardless of model, originality or type so always need to be carried out. Start with the overview to asess whether it is more or less all there, the general condition and whether it excites you or produces a feeling of dread. If the latter, then say farewell and go on your way; you will never be happy with it even after an expensive rebuild.

Next, check it in detail from stem to stern. Inspect the tyres, try to rock the wheels and feel how they turn, look for play in front and rear suspension, see if the headstock is tight or loose once the damper is slack and check

the suspension for movement, noise and damping.

Look over the cycle parts for splits and cracks as these will need welding and then refinishing. See if there are dents in the

The RRT stamped on the shell is a nice find but the only way to be sure about the ratios inside is to take it apart and count all the gear teeth. Same applies if STD is the marking.

The fierce A65H of 1966 sold mainly in the USA as the Hornet, built solely for off-road enduro work. The weight and power take some holding.

The line-up for 1970 with singles, twins and the triple. Included is the Bushman Bantam and the Military B40, but who could have seen the firm collapsing within such a short time.

The 1970 Rocket 3 with its ray gun silencers and the bellcrank twin leading shoe front brake, which had to cope with the power, speed and weight of this fast motorcycle.

tanks as these could be expensive to correct, inspect the underside of the petrol tank for signs of leaks or attempts to mend same. See if the brakes work at all and whether the spokes need replacement. Check the controls and switches to see if they work easily and correctly or are either stiff and corroded or sloppy and worn out.

Finally, inspect the engine and gearbox. Look over both for oil leaks, signs of an excess of jointing compound and cracked or broken fins or lugs. See if the chains are in good order and adjustment and then ask the owner to start up the machine. If there is a refusal or a feeble excuse, either be on your way or drastically revise your opening offer. There is no reason why any BSA, even a Gold Star, should not start easily and run nicely. Learn how they sound before you go

shopping and allow for an all-alloy engine to rattle only a little more than an iron one.

Expect the drive to take up smoothly and the gears to change quickly and easily. If they refuse to do this, either there is a gearbox problem, so you cannot ride the machine, or the clutch needs attention.

If you have the chance to ride the machine on the road, or be a passenger, expect it to run in a happy manner. They do normally, so if you find one that does not this indicates a need for some adjustment as a minimum and maybe major work. Even if it is only a matter of a minor correction, the fact that the seller has not bothered is a clear indication of attitude. While out on the road try to see if the wheels run in line as they should, as this could indicate trouble or confirm a good buy if all is well.

Later days and a club outing with the rare Fury twin alongside the late-type Rocket 3, both with the conical front hub with doubtful brake.

Happier times, with dealers in the USA being shown the scooter twin flanked by the more interesting Rocket Scrambler and other twins.

Identification

In addition to the general checks, there are more specific checks to be made and the paperwork which come together in some cases. To start with, the engine and frame numbers *must* be taken from the machine and *must* be checked against those shown in the registration documents. In the United Kingdom this is the V5 and if one is not forthcoming it may well be that the machine is not registered and not entitled to the number plate it carries.

These numbers must be checked or there could be problems in the future. In the United Kingdom, if there is no V5 you will have to apply for one with proof of ownership of the machine and a dating letter to confirm the age of the model. If all is well it will then be issued with an age-related mark, and if not with a number with a letter Q prefix. Either will devalue it to a degree in its home country where the original number is often held in high esteem, but procedures in other countries differ.

The next stage is to compare the numbers with those given in the appendices in this book, bearing in mind that the model year runs from the previous August. So, a 1955 model, for example, could be built, sold and then registered before the end of 1954. From 1969 the firm used a code system to date the models and the two letters give both month and year. Be careful with these because they again run from August to July, and the second letter for the year functions over this model year.

This code tells you what the machine *should* be, but you now need to confirm that it *is* what it claims. For this, you use the identity charts given in the appendices to check out the external features for the model in question. If any one is not there, or not as it should be, look through the charts to see which model it has come from. Where necessary, refer also to the general text but in most cases the chart should cover all that you can inspect of a complete machine.

The internals are another matter, but if the outside checks out well there is a good chance that the interior will also. However, always remember that it is only too easy to change parts around in the engine so be extra careful with the sports models. The gearbox is another area that may not be what it seems, and even when it is marked RRT2 it can still have standard ratios inside. A road test may give an idea on this, but the only way to be sure is to take the gears out and count the teeth on each one. It is also not a help to find hot cams in a cooking engine as they are unlikely to help it, and be wary of a sports engine with a high compression ratio that has acquired an iron cylinder head, for it is bound to overheat and may seize.

One further check can be the finish and colours which are also given in the appendices. The patina of age on an original finish can be detected quite easily as can a new coat of paint. If the colours do not check out, this may not be too serious but it is another factor to take into account with your overall assessment.

If the machine is not all standard you have to decide how important this is to you, which will depend on your intended use. For general riding it will not matter much and the changes may well be desirable improvements. If you are going to show the machine, however, they can be more important and in this case a judgment has to be made as to the effect and ease of correction. Some detail parts may be simple enough to replace with originals, but others could prove impossible.

Negotiations

Negotiations can be short or protracted. It may be a case of a price without negotiation or a conversation that continues for months before a deal is finally struck. Fortunately for most of us the middle course prevails and an equitable price is arrived at without too much delay.

There is no negotiation in the normal sense at an auction where you have to decide on your limit and stick to it. Only if the machine fails to reach its reserve are you likely to be able to do a private deal.

When buying from a dealer or a private owner there will normally be a stated asking price. This may be viewed as a starting point and represents the highest value the owner has dared to pitch to without losing all response to his advert or whatever. This may state that the price is not negotiable, but most are, especially when faced with a pile of crisp bank notes.

The price may have the letters "ono," "ovno" or "bo" alongside it, which stand for "or near offer," "or very near offer" or "best offer" and indicate that the owner is prepared to barter to an extent. How much may often be gauged from the figure and thus £650 ono most likely means that £600 would be highly acceptable and maybe as much as was really expected. On the other hand, £650 ovno means you offer £600 and settle at the split on £625. A quick survey of a recent magazine will give many more examples of this type.

Just as the asking price is the highest that the seller hopes to get, so your first offer is the lowest you are going to buy at. Think long and hard before coming out with a figure, for it will be nearly impossible to reduce it later. The only chance of this is if some undisclosed fact comes to light during the discussion. But even this will not do much to strengthen your position.

First ask yourself whether you really want the model, whether it fits your needs and if the one you are looking at is the right machine. It may be fitted with a number of options which the seller will claim greatly enhances its value and, while this may be true, they only count if you really want them. Thus the optional plunger frame of the early singles and twins could become a defect if you really want a machine with rigid frame.

If you finally decide that you have found just the machine for you, run through your notes for faults to criticise and features that are nonstandard or not wanted. Work out the figure you could be happy at and then go down to your first silly offer.

This may be greeted with derision, but it is a start and the ball is now with the seller who can either say no way or suggest another figure. Keep at it, but remember that you may not be alone in reading these words!

The deal

All being well you should arrive at a price with the seller in due course. This may involve a trade-in with a dealer, although this is less usual with the older machines, and your calculations must take all this into account.

Once you have paid for the machine it is your responsibility which means you need to insure it. Even if you do not intend to ride it on the road immediately you should arrange coverage against fire or theft. It will be best to go to a specialist broker who can arrange coverage on an agreed value basis to reflect what the model is worth. The coverage for road use may also be on a restricted mileage basis, which will be more suited to the use that most owners will have.

When you pay for the machine, do get a receipt that covers details, registration mark, and engine and frame numbers. Also, in the United Kingdom, collect the V5 and MoT documents, if there are any, and any other material on the machine such as parts list, owners handbook or instruction manual.

Check that they are relevant to the model and year; if not they will need replacement.

The next problem you will have is to transport the machine home, since you can ride it only if all the documentation is in order and you have your riding gear with you. Often it will mean using a van or a car and trailer unless the seller can assist.

The golden rule

If you are not totally happy about the machine, leave it to someone else and walk away. Make sure you know what "totally happy" is for you regardless of what others think, machine value or investment rating. If the machine *really* is the one you want, then have it and enjoy it to the full, whether Bantam or B31, C10 or Rocket 3, Royal Star or Firebird Scrambler.

Engine and frame numbers

Until 1968, BSA used a numbering system with a distinctive prefix for each type of machine, so it is easy to see if the engine and frame are from the same model or not. They then turned to a system using a dating code which was common to all models. The engine and frame number of the first arrangement seldom match, but may in some cases, while they should match in the second. Some engines carry extra letters such as P for police and HC for high compression.

The bulk of the numbers given are for postwar machines, but those applying to the wartime M20 are included. These machines were built with matching engine and frame numbers but when they underwent a major service there was no attempt made to keep them together, so they seldom match now. Some data on the system used in the 1930s is included and also the series used by the Ariel Huntmaster 646 cc twin, in case you find one in your BSA frame.

Prewar models

From 1932–35 BSA used a system based on numbering the annual model range from 1 upward, plus a prefix letter for the model type. The engines during this period used a combination of a year letter and the range number. Thus for 1933 the range number began at 1 for the 249 cc side-valve single and ran up to 13 for the 1000 cc vee-twin.

The first was thus the B33–1 and the last the G33–13, having been the G32–10 the year before and becoming the G34–14 the following year, when the range size increased.

For 1936 the year numbers were left out, and from 1937 the system was amended. From then the engine and frame used the year letter followed by the model type and the actual number. This followed through for all engines, but the frames differed a little as some were used for more than one model so the one prefix was common to several. Thus the 1937 M20 numbers began from engine HM20–101 and frame HM19–101 with the same frame also being used by four other models. The year letters were: 1932=Z, 1933=A, 1934=B, 1935=E, 1936=D, 1937=H, 1938=J, 1939=K and 1940=W.

Wartime models

The wartime M20 models have a letter W prefix as used for the few 1940 machines which were built between the works returning from their annual holiday and the outbreak of war. Approximate dates of production are as follows:

1939	101–9719
1940	9720–27039
1941	27040–50549
1942	50550–70000
1943	70001–90000
1944	90001–110000
1945	110001 on

Postwar models 1945–69

Bantam

Year	Model	Engine		Rigid frame	Spring frame
		Wipac	*Lucas*		
1949	D1	UYD–101			
	D1	YD–101		YD1–101	
1950	D1	UYD–20001	UYDL–101		
	D1	YD–20001	YDL–101	YD1–20001	YD1S–20001
1951	D1	YD1–40001	YDL1–3001	YD1–40001	YD1S–40001
1952	D1	YD1–63001	YDL1–8001	YD1–64001	YD1S–64001
1953	D1	BD2–101	BD2L–101	BD2–101	BD2S–101

Year	Model	Engine		Rigid frame	Spring frame
		Direct/ competition	*Battery*		
1954	D1	BD–101	BDB–101	BD2–14600	BD2S–14600
	D3	BD3–101	BD3B–101	BD2–14600	BD2S–14600
1955	D1	DD–101	DDB–101	BD2–34701	BD2S–34701
	D3	BD3–5138	BD3B–5138	BD2–34701	BD2S–34701

Year	Model	Engine		Plunger frame
		Direct	*Battery*	
1956	D1	DD–4801	DDB–3301	BD2S–55001
1957	D1	DD–	DDB–	BD2S–
1958	D1	DD–8577	DDB–7849	BD2S–65001
1959	D1	DD–10812	DDB–10628	BD2S–67581
1960	D1	DD–12501	DDB–12501	BD2S–70501
1961	D1	DD–14501	DDB–14501	BD2S–73701
1962	D1	DD–15481	DDB–16413	BD2S–76680
1963	D1	DD–16129	DDB–17606	BD2S–78746

Year	Model	Engine		Swing arm frame
		Direct	*Battery*	
1956	D3	BD3–10401	BD3B–12801	CD3–101
1957	D3	BD3–	BD3B–	CD3–
1958	D5	ED5–101	ED5B–101	FD5–101
1959	D7	ED7–101	ED7B–101	D7–101
1960	D7	ED7–1501	ED7B–7001	D7–8101
1961	D7	ED7–3001	ED7B–15501	D7–18401
1962	D7	ED7–4501	ED7B–23001	D7–27450
1963	D7	ED7–5505	ED7B–26904	D7–33268
	D7 (Police)		ED7BP–26904	D7–33268
	D7A (USA)	ED7A–5505	ED7BA–26904	D7–33268
	D7 (Trail)	ED7–5505		D7–33268T
1964	D7	ED7–6887	FD7–101	D7–38400
	D7 (USA)	ED7A–6887	FD7A–101	D7–38400
	D7 (Trail)	ED7–6887		D7–38400
1965	D7	ED7–9001	FD7–3001	D7–42878
1966	D7 (de luxe)	FD7–101	FD7–9076	D7–49855 to 51960; GD7–101 to 8616
	D7 Silver	FD7–101	FD7–10127	D7–51320 to 51960; GD7–101 to 8616

Bantam

Year	Model	Engine	Swing arm frame
1967	D10	D10–101	D10–101
	D10S Sports	D10A–101	D10A–101
	D10B Bushman	D10A–101	BD10A–101
1968	D14/4 Supreme	D13B–101 to 780	D13B–101
	D14/4S Sports	D13B–101 to 780	D13B–101S
	D14/4B Bushman	D13C–101 to 780	D13C–101B
	D14/4 Supreme	D14B–781	D14B–781
	D14/4S Sports	D14B–781	D14B–781S
	D14/4B Bushman	D14C–781	D14C–781B

C range
C10 and C11

Year	C10 engine	C11 engine	Rigid frame	Spring frame
1946–47	XC10–101	XC11–101	XC10G–101 Girders	
			XC10T–101 Telescopics	
1948	YC10–101	YC11–101	YC10–101	
1949	ZC10–101	ZC11–101	ZC10–101	
1950	ZC10–4001	ZC11–8001	ZC10–10001	
1951	ZC10–7001	ZC11–16001	ZC10–21001	ZC10S–101
	With four-speed gearbox			ZC10S4–101
1952	ZC10–10001	ZC11–25001	ZC10–29001	ZC10S–2601
	With four-speed gearbox			ZC10S4–2001
1953	BC10–101	BC11–101	BC10–101	BC10S–101
	With four-speed gearbox			BC10S4–101

C10L, C11G and C12

Year	Model	Engine	Rigid frame	Spring frame
1954	C10L	BC10L–101		BC10LS–101
	C11G	BC11G–101	BC11–101	BC11S–101
	C11G (4-speed)	BC11G–101	BC11R4–101	BC11S4–101
1955	C10L	BC10L–4001		BC10LS–4501
	C11G	BC11G–11501	BC11–801	BC11S–4001
	C11G (4-speed)	BC11G–11501	BC11R4–501	BC11S4–8001
1956	C10L	BC10L–7001		DC10S–101
	C12	BC11G–23001		EC12–101
				BC11S4–18001
1957	C10L	BC10L–		DC10S–
	C12	BC11G–		EC12–
1958	C12	BC11G–40001		EC12–16001

B range
B31 and B33

Year	B31 engine	B33 engine	Rigid frame	Spring frame
1946	XB31–101		XB31–101	
1947	XB31–101	XB33–101	XB31–101	
1948	YB31–101	YB33–101	YB31–101	
1949	ZB31–101	ZB33–101	ZB31–101	ZB31S–101
1950	ZB31–9001	ZB33–4001	ZB31–9001	ZB31S–5001
1951	ZB31–15001	ZB33–7001	ZB31–14001	ZB31S–10001
1952	ZB31–21001	ZB33–11001	ZB31–19001	ZB31S–17001
1953	BB31–101	BB33–101	BB31–101	BB31S–101
1954	BB31–6001	BB33–2001	BB31–1386	BB31S–5895
	BB31–6001	BB33–2001		CB31–101
1955	BB31–15001	BB33–5001		BB31S–12001
	BB31–15001	BB33–5001		CB31–6001

B range

B31 and B33

Year	B31 engine	B33 engine	Rigid frame	Spring frame
1956	BB31-22001	BB33-7301		EB31-101
1957	BB31-	BB33-		EB31-
1958	GB31-101	GB33-101		FB31-101
1959	GB31-1909	GB33-662		FB31-2572
1960		GB33-1001		GB33-101

B32 and B34

Year	B32 engine	B34 engine	Rigid frame	Spring frame
1946	XB32-101		XB31-101	
1947	XB32-101	XB34-101	XB31-101	
1948	YB32-101	YB34-101	YB31-101	
1949	ZB32-101	ZB34-101	ZB31-101	
1950	ZB32-3001	ZB34-2001	ZB31-9001	ZB31S-5001
Alloy	ZB32A-3001	ZB34A-2001	ZB31-9001	ZB31S-5001
1951	ZB32-4001	ZB34-3001	ZB31-14001	ZB31S-10001
Alloy	ZB32A-4001	ZB34A-3001	ZB31-14001	ZB31S-10001
1952	ZB32-5001	ZB34-4001	ZB31-19001	ZB31S-17001
Alloy	ZB32A-5001		ZB31-19001	ZB31S-17001
Sand cast		ZB34A-4001	ZB31-19001	ZB31S-17001
Diecast		ZB34A-5001	ZB31-19001	ZB31S-17001
1953	BB32A-101	BB34A-101	BB31-101	BB31S-101
1954	BB32A-201	BB34A-201	BB32R-12	CB31-101
1955	BB32A-251	BB34A-301	BB32A-201	
1956	BB32A-301	BB34A-351		CB34-101
1957	BB32A-	BB34A-		CB34-

Gold Star B32 and B34

Year	B32 engine	B34 engine	Rigid frame	Spring frame
1949	ZB32GS-101	ZB34GS-101	ZB31-101	ZB32S-101
1950	ZB32GS-2001	ZB34GS-2001	ZB31-9001	ZB32S-2001
1951	ZB32GS-3001	ZB34GS-3001	ZB31-14001	ZB32S-3001
1952	ZB32GS-4001		ZB31-19001	ZB32S-4001
Clubman	ZB32GS-6001		ZB31-19001	ZB32S-4001
Sand cast		ZB34GS-4001	ZB31-19001	ZB32S-4001
Diecast		ZB34GS-5001	ZB31-19001	ZB32S-4001
1953	BB32GS-101	BB34GS-101	BB31-101	BB32S-101
	BB32GS-101	BB34GS-101		BB32A-101 (Swing arm)
1954	BB32GS-1001	BB34GS-1001		CB32-101
	CB32GS-101	CB34GS-101		CB32-101
Daytona		BB34GSD-101	CB32D-101	
1955	BB32GS-2001	BB34GS-2001		CB32-1501
	CB32GS-501	CB34GS-501		CB32-1501
	DB32GS-101	DB34GS-101		CB32-4001
1956		DB34GS-501	BB32R-301	

Year	B32 engine	B34 engine	B34 DBD engine	Spring frame
1956	DB32GS-501	DB34GS-501	DBD34GS-2001	CB32-4001
1957	DB32GS-	DB34GS-	DBD34GS-2963	CB32-
1958			DBD34GS-3001	CB32-7001

Year	B32 engine	B34 engine	Spring frame	Catalina frame
1959	DB32GS-1501	DBD34GS-3753	CB32-7873	CB32C-101
1960	DB32GS-1601	DBD34GS-4601	CB32-8701	CB32C-351
1961	DB32GS-1741	DBD34GS-5684	CB32-10101	CB32C-601
1962	DB32GS-1794	DBD34GS-6504	CB32-11001	CB32C-741
1963		DBD34GS-6881	CB32-11451	CB32C-857

Note: Catalina models used 499 cc engine only.

M range

Year	M20 engine	M21 engine	M33 engine	Rigid frame	Spring frame
1946–47	XM20–101	XM21–101		XM20–101	
1948	YM20–101	YM21–101	YM33–101	YM20–101	
1949	ZM20–101	ZM21–101	ZM33–101	ZM20–101	
1950	ZM20–4001	ZM21–5001	ZM33–3001	ZM20–7001	
1951	ZM20–6001	ZM21–8001	ZM33–4001	ZM20–10001	ZM20S–101
1952	ZM20–10001	ZM21–10001	ZM33–5001	ZM20–14001	ZM20S–301
1953	BM20–101	BM21–101	BM33–101	BM20–101	BM20S–101
1954	BM20–1001	BM21–1601	BM33–501	BM20–1502	BM20S–1192
1955	BM20–2501	BM21–4501	BM33–1301	BM20–4001	BM20S–4001
1956		BM21–7501	BM33–2101	BM20–7001	BM20S–8001
1957		BM21–	BM33–	BM20–	BM20S–
1958		BM21–11001		BM20–10001	BM20S–11001
1959		BM21–12033		BM20–10313	BM20S–12031
1960		BM21–12901		BM20–10451	BM20S–12031
1961		BM21–14301			BM20S–14201
1962		BM21–15453			BM20S–15061
1963		BM21–15588			BM20S–15159

Note: For 1961–63 some M21 engines had an alternator fitted. Where this was done a letter A was added to the engine number prefix.

C15 range

Year	C15 engine	SS80 engine	Frame
1959	C15–101		C15–101
1960	C15–11001		C15–11101
1961	C15–21251		C15–22001
		C15SS–101	C15–27644
1962	C15–29839	C15SS–1101	C15–31801
1963	C15–41807	C15SS–2705	C15–38035
1964	C15D–101	C15SS–3633	C15–42211
1965	C15F–101	C15FSS–101	C15–45501

Year	C15 engine	Sportsman engine	Frame
1966	C15F–2089	C15FSS–2001	C15–49001
1967	C15G–101		C15G–101
		C15SG–101	C15SG–101

C15 competition range

Year	C15S engine	C15T engine	Frame
1959	C15S–101	C15T–101	C15S–101
1960	C15S–301	C15T–301	C15S–501
1961	C15S–2112	C15T–1056	C15S–2701
1962	C15S–3101		C15S–3601
		C15T–1451	C15S–10001
1963	C15S–4001	C15T–2001	C15C–101
1964	C15S–4373	C15T–2116	C15C–853
1965	C15FS–101	C15FT–101	C15C–1601

Other C15 models

Year	C15 USA engine	C15 police engine	Frame
1963	C15B–409	C15P–41807	C15–38035
1964	C15DB–101	C15DP–101	C15–42211
1965	C15FB–101	C15FP–101	C15–45501
1967		C15PG–101	C15PG–101

Year	Pastoral engine	C15 Racer	Frame
1963	C15T–1602		C15A–137
		C15R–101	C15S–4123
1964	C15T–2116		C15E–101
1965	C15FT–101		C15E–136

Year	C15 Starfire	C15 Trials Cat	Frame
1963	C15–41807		C15C–101
1964	C15SR–225		C15C–853
1965	C15FSR–101	C15FT–101	C15C–1601

B40, C25, B25 and B44 ranges

Year	B40 engine	SS90 engine	Frame
1961	B40–101		B40–101
1962	B40–3601	B40BSS–101	B40–3511
1963	B40–4506	B40SS–180	B40–5017
1964	B40–5275	B40SS–426	B40–6668
1965	B40F–101	B40FSS–101	B40–7775
1966	B40F–1149		B40–9973
	B40G–101		B40–9973
1967	B40G–201		B40G–201

Model	Year	Engine	Frame
B40 (USA)	1963	B40B–563	B40–5017
B40 (Police)	1964	B40P–5275	B40–6668
	1965	B40FP–101	B40–7775
B40 Super Star	1964	B40B–1088	B40–6668
B40 Sportsman	1965	B40FB–101	B40–7775
B40 Enduro Star	1964	B40T–143	C15C–853
	1965	B40FE–101	C15C–1601
B40 Rough Rider	1969	HCB40–462M	HCB40–462M
C25	1967	C25–101	C25–101
B25	1967	C25–101	B25–101
	1968	B25B–101	B25B–101
B44GP	1966	B44–101	B44–101
	1967	B44–131	B44–267
B44VE	1966	B44E–101	C15C–3137
	1967	B44EA–101	B44EA–101
B44VR	1967	B44R–101	B44R–101
B44SS	1968	B44B–101	B44B–101SS
B44VS	1968	B44B–101	B44B–101VS

Semi- and pre-unit twins

Year	A7 engine	A7ST engine	A10 engine	Rigid frame	Plunger frame
1947	XA7–101			XA7–101	
1948	YA7–101			YA7–101	
1949	ZA7–101	ZA7S–101		ZA7–101	ZA7S–101
1950	ZA7–7001	ZA7S–4001	ZA10–101	ZA7–4001	ZA7S–6001
1951	AA7–101	AA7S–101	ZA10–4001	ZA7–6001	ZA7S–14001
1952	AA7–5001	AA7S–1001	ZA10–12001	ZA7–8001	ZA7S–26001
1953	BA7–101	BA7S–101	BA10–101	BA7–101	BA7S–101
1954	BA7–2001	BA7S–2001	BA10–7001		BA7S–8950
1955			BA10–11001		BA7S–15001
1956			BA10–14001		BA7S–18001
1957			BA10–16036 (Last)		BA7S–20289

Year	A7 engine	A7SS engine	A10 engine	A10RR engine	Swing arm frame
1954	CA7-101	CA7SS-101	CA10-101	CA10R-101	CA7-101
1955	CA7-1501	CA7SS-501	CA10-4501	CA10R-601	CA7-7001
1956	CA7-2701	CA7SS-2301	CA10-8001	CA10R-2001	EA7-101
1957	CA7-	CA7SS-	CA10-	CA10R-	EA7-
1958	CA7-5001	CA7SS-4501	DA10-651	CA10R-6001	FA7-101
1959	CA7-5867	CA7SS-5425	DA10-4616	CA10R-8193	FA7-8522
1960	CA7-7101	CA7SS-6701	DA10-7801	DA10R-101	GA7-101
1961	CA7-8501	CA7SS-8001	DA10-13201	DA10R-3001	GA7-11101
1962	CA7-9714	CA7SS-9277	DA10-17181	DA10R-5958	GA7-21120
1963			DA10-17727	DA10R-8197	GA7-23643

Note: From 1961 some engines were fitted with an alternator and the engine number prefix would then have a letter A added to it. From 1958 the sports A10 model was the A10SR.

A10 Super Flash, Spitfire and RGS

Year	Engine	SF frame	Spitfire frame	RGS frame
1953	BA10S-101	BA10-101		
1954	BA10S-701	BA10S-701		
1959	CA10SR-776		FA7A-101	
1960	DA10SR-101		GA7A-101	
1961	DA10SR-401		GA7A-401	
1962	DA10R-5958		GA7A-536	GA10-101
1963	DA10R-8197		GA7A-748	GA10-390
Last RGS	DA10R-10388			GA10-1914

Unit twins

Model	1962	1963	1964	1965
A50	A50-101	A50-823	A50A-101	A50A-686
A50 (Police)			A50AP-101	A50AP-121
A65	A65-101	A65-1947	A65A-101	A65A-1134
A65 (Police)			A65AP-101	A65AP-267
A65R			A65B-101	A65B-334
A65R (Rev-counter)			A65C-101	A65C-1082
A65T/R			A65B-101	
Model above frame	A50-101	A50-2288	A50-5501	A50-8437
Above rod brake	A50A-101	A50-2701		
Model below frame			A50B-101	A50B-4001
A50C (USA)			A50B-101	A50D-101
A65L/R			A65D-101	A65D-1742
A65SH			A65E-101	A65E-701
A50CC (USA)				A50B-507
A50C and A50CC (UK)				A50DC-101
A65L and A65LC				A65DC-2158

Model	1966	1967	1968	1969
A50 Royal Star	A50R-101	A50RA-101	A50RB-101	A50RC-101
A50 Wasp	A50W-101	A50WA-101	A50WB-101	
A65 Thunderbolt	A65T-101	A65TA-101	A65TB-101	A65TC-101
A65 Lightning	A65L-101	A65LA-101	A65LB-101	A65LC-101
A65 Hornet	A65H-101	A65HA-101		
A65 Firebird			A65FB-101	A65FC-101
A65 Spitfire	A65S-101	A65SA-101	A65SB-101	
Frame number	A50C-101	As engine	As engine	As engine

1969 and later

From 1969 on, a new coding system was used with a two-letter prefix for the month and model season year, followed by the model code and a serial number. This last began each year at 00101 and ran on irrespective of the machine it went on. The model season year ran from August to July.

The first letter was the month and the code was:

A	January	E	May	K	September
B	February	G	June	N	October
C	March	H	July	P	November
D	April	J	August	X	December

The second letter was the model year and the code was:

C August 1968 to July 1969
D August 1969 to July 1970
E August 1970 to July 1971
G August 1971 to July 1972
H August 1972 to July 1973

Model codes were:
1969–70 D175, D175B, B25S, B44SS, B44VS, A50R, A65T, A65L, A65F, A75
1971 D175, B25SS, B25T, A65FS
1971–72 B50SS, B50T, A65T, A65L, A75, A75V
1971–73 B50MX
1972 A70L

Scooters

Year	Single engine	Twin engine	Frame
1959		W101	101B
1960	S–101	W3201	4001
1961	S–6720	W11790	18800B
1962	S–11407	W17800	30140B
1963	S–12498	W18485	31825B
1964	S–13263		33661B
1965	S–13576		34300B

Note: Electric start twins had letter E added to engine number.

Dandy and Beagle

Year	Dandy engine	Dandy frame
1957	DSE–101	DS–101
1958	DSE–11001	DS–11501
1959	DSE–14462	DS–15165
1960	DSE–17901	DS–18001
1961	DSE–21651	DS–21801
1962	DSE–22164	DS–22268

Year	Beagle engine	Beagle frame
1964	K1–101	K1–101
1965	K1–3507	K1–3315

Ariel Huntmaster

Year	Engine prefix
1954	PJ
1955	LF
1956	MLF
1957	NLF 2858
1958	CNLF 4230
1959	CNLF 5838
Last	CNLF 6073

BSA identity and model range charts

The identity charts list external features and are provided as a guide and checklist when viewing a potential purchase. Engine and frame numbers remain the first point to check *always*. But after that the features can give a good indication as to whether the machine is what it says it is, or is from another year or a hybrid.

The list of features for each model was first developed in an attempt to isolate a unique set for each year as a basis for checking. Many items appear for several models as they were common to the range, but are included each time where they can help. The list was then expanded a little to include points that are often of interest, even when they may not help with dating. This may mean that for one particular year there are several points that changed, but all are included since they all should be there if the machine is original.

All the external features listed can be checked without dismantling. The internal changes are of no help when you are looking, but remember that they may be far reaching due to the ease with which parts may be switched around among models in some ranges. When going to view, make a list of points to check, but take this book as well. It will help establish where any rogue parts have come from.

The model range charts come automatically from the identity charts, which give the years for which each model was built. These are also covered in the rating box at the start of each machine range chapter, and all are for the model year rather than the calendar year. The new season's models were built from August on to be ready for the November show and distribution to the dealers, hence the distinction.

Winged Wheel	**Model year**		
Feature	'53	'54	'55
wheel alone	*	*	*
complete machine listed			*

Beagle	**Model year**	
Feature	'64	'65
listed	*	*

Dandy	**Model year**					
Feature	'57	'58	'59	'60	'61	'62
listed	*	*	*	*	*	*

Bantam

D1, rigid, Wipac

Feature	'48	'49	'50	'51	'52	'53	'54	'55
Geni-mag	*	*						
Wipac mag			*	*	*	*	*	*
stand clip	*	*						
stand spring			*	*	*	*	*	*
flat silencer	*	*	*	*	*	*		
tubular silencer							*	*
shovel guard	*	*	*	*	*			
bar switch	*	*	*	*				
lamp cowl							*	*
small fins	*	*	*	*	*	*		
large fins							*	*
saddle	*	*	*	*	*	*	*	*
dualseat option						*	*	*

D1, plunger, Wipac

Feature	'50	'51	'52	'53	'54	'55
Wipac mag	*	*	*	*	*	*
stand spring	*	*	*	*	*	*
flat silencer	*	*	*	*		
tubular silencer					*	*
shovel guard	*	*	*			
lamp cowl					*	*
bar switch	*	*				
small fins	*	*	*	*		
large fins					*	*
saddle	*	*	*	*	*	*
dualseat option				*	*	*

D1, rigid or plunger, Lucas

Feature	'50	'51	'52	'53
stand spring	*	*	*	*
flat silencer	*	*	*	*
shovel guard	*	*	*	
small fins	*	*	*	*
saddle	*	*	*	*
dualseat option				*

D1, rigid, battery

Feature	'54	'55
Wipac mag	*	*
stand spring	*	*
tubular silencer	*	*
lamp cowl	*	*
large fins	*	*
saddle	*	*
dualseat option	*	*

D1, plunger, direct or battery

Feature	'54	'55	'56	'57	'58	'59	'60	'61	'62	'63
Wipac mag	*	*	*	*	*	*	*	*	*	*
stand spring	*	*	*	*	*	*	*	*	*	*
tubular silencer	*	*	*	*	*	*	*	*	*	*
lamp cowl	*	*	*	*	*	*	*	*	*	*
large fins	*	*	*	*	*	*	*	*	*	*
saddle	*	*	*	*	*	*	*	*	*	*
dualseat option	*	*	*	*	*	*	*	*	*	*

D1, competition, rigid or plunger, Wipac

Feature	'50	'51	'52	'53	'54	'55
flat silencer	*	*	*	*	*	*
bar switch	*	*				
small fins	*	*	*	*		
large fins					*	*
raised saddle	*	*	*	*	*	*
decompressor	*	*	*	*	*	*
folding kickstart	*	*	*	*	*	*
rigid frame	*	*	*	*	*	*
plunger frame	*	*	*	*	*	

D1, competition, rigid or plunger, Lucas

Feature	'50	'51	'52	'53
stand spring	*	*	*	*
flat silencer	*	*	*	*
small fins	*	*	*	*
saddle	*	*	*	*

D3, plunger and swing arm, direct or battery

Feature	Model year			
	'54	'55	'56	'57
plunger frame	*	*		
swing-arm frame			*	*
tubular silencer	*	*		
long silencer			*	*
lamp cowl	*	*	*	*
large fins	*	*	*	*
saddle	*	*		
dualseat option	*	*		
dualseat			*	*

D3, competition, rigid and plunger

Feature	Model year	
	'54	'55
rigid frame	*	*
plunger frame	*	
flat silencer	*	*
large fins	*	*
saddle	*	*

D5, swing arm, direct and battery

Feature	Model year
	'58
wider brakes	*
deep tank	*

D7 Super

Feature	Model year						
	'59	'60	'61	'62	'63	'64	'65
flange carb	*	*	*	*	*	*	*
generator cover	*	*	*	*	*	*	*
nacelle	*	*	*	*	*	*	*
twin switches						*	*

D7 Super de luxe, Silver and De Luxe

Feature	Model year		
	'64	'65	'66
flange carb	*	*	*
generator cover	*	*	*
nacelle	*	*	*
twin switches	*	*	*
tank recesses (Silver and De Luxe)			*

D10 Silver and Supreme

Feature	Model year	
	'66	'67
3 speeds	*	*
Monobloc	*	
Concentric	*	*
points on right	*	*
nacelle	*	*
offset hubs	*	*

D10S Sports

Feature	Model year	
	'66	'67
4 speeds	*	*
Monobloc	*	
Concentric	*	*
points on right	*	*
headlamp shell	*	*
full-width hubs	*	*
waist exhaust	*	*
flyscreen	*	*
dualseat hump	*	*
no rear unit covers	*	*

D10B Bushman

Feature	Model year	
	'66	'67
4 speeds	*	*
Monobloc	*	
Concentric	*	*
points on right	*	*
headlamp shell	*	*
offset hubs	*	*
raised exhaust	*	*
undershield	*	*
no rear unit covers	*	*

D14/4 Supreme

Feature	Model year
	'68
large exhaust	*
4 speeds	*
rest as D10 Supreme	*

D14/4S Sports

Feature	Model year
	'68
large exhaust	*
rest as D10S	*

D14/4B Bushman

Feature	'68
large exhaust	*
full-width front	*
offset rear	*
rest as D10B	*

D175

Feature	'69	'70	'71
centre plug	*	*	*
large exhaust	*	*	*
4 speeds	*	*	*
Concentric	*	*	*
points on right	*	*	*
headlamp shell	*	*	*
offset hubs	*	*	*
low exhaust	*	*	*
rear unit covers	*	*	*

D175B Bushman

Feature	'69	'70
centre plug	*	*
large exhaust	*	*
4 speeds	*	*
Concentric	*	*
points on right	*	*
headlamp shell	*	*
offset hubs	*	*
raised exhaust	*	*
undershield	*	*
no rear unit covers	*	*

Scooter

B1

Feature	'59	'60	'61	'62	'63	'64	'65
listed	*	*	*	*	*	*	*

B2 and B2S

Feature	'59	'60	'61	'62	'63	'64
listed	*	*	*	*	*	*

C range

C10 and C11

Feature	'45	'46	'47	'48	'49	'50	'51	'52	'53
rigid frame	*	*	*	*	*	*	*	*	*
plunger frame							*	*	*
girder forks	*	*							
telescopic forks		*	*	*	*	*	*	*	*
speedo in tank		*	*	*	*	*	*	*	
3 speeds	*	*	*	*	*	*	*	*	*
4 speeds							*	*	*
alloy head C10					*	*	*	*	*
dualseat option									*
20 in. wheels C11	*	*	*	*	*	*	*		
drip shield C11				*					
de luxe C11 model				*	*	*	*		

C10L

Feature	'54	'55	'56	'57
plunger frame	*	*	*	*
alternator	*	*	*	*
3 speeds	*	*		
4 speeds			*	*
fork cowl	*	*	*	*
Monobloc		*	*	*
twin switches			*	*

C11G and C12

Feature	'54	'55	'56	'57	'58
rigid frame	*				
plunger frame	*	*			
swing-arm frame			*	*	*
alternator	*	*	*	*	*
3 speeds	*	*			
4 speeds	*	*	*	*	*
fork cowl	*	*	*	*	*
Monobloc		*	*	*	*
7 in. front brake		*	*	*	*
full-width hubs			*	*	*

B range
B31 and B33

Feature	'45	'46	'47	'48	'49	'50	'51	'52	'53	'54	'55
rigid frame	*	*	*	*	*	*	*	*	*	*	
plunger frame					*	*	*	*	*	*	*
speedo in tank	*	*	*								
saddle	*	*	*	*	*	*	*	*	*	*	*
dualseat option								*	*	*	*
alloy engine option						*					
headlamp cowl									*	*	*
B33 listed			*	*	*	*	*	*	*	*	*
B33 8 in. front brake									*	*	*
B33 valanced front guard									*	*	*

B31 and B33

Feature	'54	'55	'56	'57	'58	'59	'60
B31 listed	*	*	*	*	*	*	
swing-arm frame	*	*	*	*	*	*	*
dualseat	*	*	*	*	*	*	*
lamp cowl	*	*	*	*			
nacelle					*	*	*
Monobloc		*		*	*	*	*
full-width hubs			*	*	*	*	*
alloy hubs			*	*			
rear chaincase option			*		*	*	*
alternator					*	*	*
coil ignition					*	*	*

B32 and B34

Feature	'46	'47	'48	'49	'50	'51	'52	'53	'54	'55	'56	'57
rigid frame	*	*	*	*	*	*	*	*	*	*		
rigid duplex frame									*	*		
plunger frame				*	*	*	*	*				
swing-arm frame									*	*	*	*
21 in. front wheel	*	*	*	*	*	*	*	*	*	*	*	*
speedo in tank	*	*										
undershield	*	*	*	*	*	*	*	*	*	*	*	*
raised exhaust	*	*	*	*	*	*	*	*	*	*	*	*
B34 listed		*	*	*	*	*	*	*	*	*	*	*
B32 scrambles special				*								
Gold Star engine option					*	*						
alloy engine option					*	*	*	*				
alloy engine									*	*	*	*
central oil tank										*	*	
Monobloc												*

Gold Star

Feature	'49	'50	'51	'52	'53	'54	'55	'56	'57	'58	'59	'60	'61	'62	'63
ZB models	*	*	*	*											
BB models					*	*	*								
CB models						*	*								
DB32							*	*	*		*	*	*	*	
DB34							*	*	*						
DBD model							*	*	*	*	*	*	*	*	*
plunger frame	*	*	*	*											
swing-arm frame					*	*	*	*	*	*	*	*	*	*	*
saddle	*	*	*	*											
dualseat option				*											
dualseat					*	*	*	*	*	*	*	*	*	*	*

Gold Star

Feature	'49	'50	'51	'52	'53	'54	'55	'56	'57	'58	'59	'60	'61	'62	'63
8 in. front brake		*	*	*	*	*	*	*	*						
190 mm brake							*	*	*	*	*	*	*	*	*
central oil tank for MX										*	*	*	*	*	*
tourer	*	*	*	*	*	*	*	*							
trials		*	*	*	*	*	*								
ISDT					*	*									
scrambles		*	*	*	*	*	*	*	*	*	*	*	*	*	*
road racing		*	*	*	*	*	*	*	*						
Clubman		*	*	*	*	*	*	*	*	*	*	*	*	*	*

M range

M20 and M21

Feature	'45	'46	'47	'48	'49	'50	'51	'52	'53	'54	'55
M21 listed		*	*	*	*	*	*	*	*	*	*
rigid frame	*	*	*	*	*	*	*	*	*	*	*
plunger frame							*	*	*	*	*
girder forks	*	*	*	*							
telescopics				*	*	*	*	*	*	*	*
alloy head							*	*	*	*	*
saddle	*	*	*	*	*	*	*	*	*	*	*
dualseat option								*	*	*	*
headlamp cowl									*	*	*
Monobloc											*

M21

Feature	'56	'57	'58	'59	'60	'61	'62	'63
rigid frame	*	*	*	*	*			
plunger frame	*	*	*	*	*	*	*	*
headlamp cowl	*	*						
8 in. front brake	*	*	*	*	*	*	*	*
valanced front guard	*	*	*	*	*	*	*	*
alternator option						*	*	*

M33

Feature	'48	'49	'50	'51	'52	'53	'54	'55	'56	'57
rigid frame	*	*	*	*	*	*	*	*		
plunger frame				*	*	*	*	*	*	*
girder forks	*									
telescopics	*	*	*	*	*	*	*	*	*	*
saddle	*	*	*	*	*	*	*	*	*	*
dualseat option					*	*	*	*	*	*
headlamp cowl						*	*	*	*	*
Monobloc								*	*	*
8 in. front brake									*	*
valanced front guard									*	*

Unit singles

C15

Feature	'59	'60	'61	'62	'63	'64	'65	'66	'67
rear points	*	*	*	*	*	*			
cover points							*	*	*
nacelle	*	*	*	*	*	*	*	*	*
17 in. wheels	*	*	*	*	*	*	*	*	*
full-width hubs	*	*	*	*	*	*	*	*	*
external clutch lever							*	*	*
Victor bottom half								*	*

C15S and C15T

Feature	Model year						
	'59	'60	'61	'62	'63	'64	'65
rear points	*	*	*	*	*	*	
cover points							*
undershield		*	*	*	*	*	*
upswept pipe		*	*	*	*	*	*
alloy tank				*	*	*	*
20 in. wheels		*	*	*	*	*	*
full-width hubs	*	*	*	*			
offset front hub				*	*	*	*
duplex seat tubes					*	*	*
centre oil tank					*	*	*
external clutch lever							*

SS80 and Sportsman

Feature	Model year					
	'61	'62	'63	'64	'65	'66
rear points	*	*	*	*		
cover points					*	*
nacelle	*	*	*	*	*	
separate headlamp						*
17 in. wheels	*	*	*	*	*	*
full-width hubs	*	*	*	*	*	*
external clutch lever						*
Victor bottom half						*
humped dualseat						*
Sportsman listed						*

C25 and B25

Feature	Model year			
	'67	'68	'69	'70
square-fin barrel	*	*	*	*
Concentric	*	*	*	*
7 in. brakes	*	*	*	*
tls front brake			*	*
offset front hub	*			
full-width front hub		*	*	*
fibreglass tank	*	*		
steel tank			*	*
Fleetstar listed			*	
oil warning light				*

B40

Feature	Model year						
	'61	'62	'63	'64	'65	'66	'67
no pushrod tube	*	*	*	*	*	*	*
rear points	*	*	*	*			
cover points					*	*	*
nacelle	*	*	*	*	*	*	*
18 in. wheel	*	*	*	*	*	*	*
full-width hubs	*	*	*	*	*	*	*
7 in. front brake	*	*	*	*	*	*	*
external clutch lever					*	*	*
Victor bottom half						*	*

SS90

Feature	Model year			
	'62	'63	'64	'65
no pushrod tube	*	*	*	*
rear points	*	*	*	
cover points				*
nacelle	*	*	*	*
18 in. wheels	*	*	*	*
full-width hubs	*	*	*	*
7 in. front brake	*	*	*	*
external clutch lever				*

B40E

Feature	Model year	
	'64	'65
rear points	*	
cover points		*
external clutch lever		*

B44GP

Feature	Model year		
	'65	'66	'67
oil in frame	*	*	*
alloy-plated barrel	*	*	*
7 in. front brake	*	*	*
7 in. rear brake			*
20 in. front wheel	*	*	*

B44VE

Feature	Model year	
	'66	'67
Monobloc	*	
Concentric		*
7 in. front brake	*	*
7 in. rear brake		*
offset hubs	*	*
small alloy tank	*	*
upswept exhaust	*	*

B44VS

Feature	Model year			
	'67	'68	'69	'70
square-fin barrel	*	*	*	*
Concentric	*	*	*	*
7 in. front brake	*			
8 in. front brake		*	*	*
7 in. rear brake	*	*	*	*
offset hubs	*	*	*	*
small alloy tank	*	*	*	*
raised exhaust	*	*	*	*
competition frame	*	*	*	*
small headlamp	*	*	*	*

B44VR and B44SS

Feature	Model year			
	'67	'68	'69	'70
square-fin barrel	*	*	*	*
Concentric	*	*	*	*
7 in. front brake	*			
8 in. front brake		*		
7 in. tls front brake			*	*
7 in. rear brake	*	*	*	*
18 in. wheels	*	*	*	*
offset front hub	*			
full-width front hub		*	*	*
offset rear hub	*	*	*	*
fibreglass tank	*	*		
steel tank			*	*

B25SS

Feature	Model year
	'71
oil-in-frame	*
slimline forks	*
conical hubs	*
8 in. tls front brake	*
6 in. front brake	*
18 in. front wheel	*
unsprung front guard	*

B25T

Feature	Model year
	'71
oil-in-frame	*
slimline forks	*
conical hubs	*
6 in. front brake	*
20 in. front wheel	*
sprung front guard	*

B50SS

Feature	Model year	
	'71	'72
oil-in-frame	*	*
slimline forks	*	*
conical hubs	*	*
8 in. tls front brake	*	*
18 in. front wheel	*	*
unsprung front guard	*	*

B50T

Feature	Model year	
	'71	'72
oil-in-frame	*	*
slimline forks	*	*
conical hubs	*	*
6 in. front brake	*	*
20 in. front wheel	*	*
sprung front guard	*	*

B50MX

Feature	Model year		
	'71	'72	'73
oil-in-frame	*	*	*
conical hubs	*	*	*
20 in front wheel	*	*	*
twin silencers	*	*	*

Pre-unit twins
A7 and A7ST Star Twin, early type

Feature	Model year			
	'47	'48	'49	'50
semi-unit engine	*	*	*	*
rocker box caps	*	*	*	*
rigid frame	*	*	*	*
plunger frame			*	*
speedo in tank	*			
one-piece front hub			*	*
revised gearbox				*
A7ST in plunger frame			*	*

A7 — Model year

Feature	'51	'52	'53	'54	'55	'56	'57	'58	'59	'60	'61	'62
semi-unit engine	*	*	*	*								
pre-unit engine					*	*	*	*	*	*	*	*
rigid frame	*											
plunger frame	*	*	*	*								
swing-arm frame					*	*	*	*	*	*	*	*
dualseat option		*	*	*								
dualseat					*	*	*	*	*	*	*	*
headlamp cowl			*	*	*	*	*					
nacelle								*	*	*	*	*
underslung pilot		*	*	*								
steering lock						*	*	*	*	*	*	*
Monobloc						*	*	*	*	*	*	*
offset hubs	*	*	*	*	*							
full-width hubs						*	*	*	*	*	*	*
alloy hubs						*	*					
7 in. front brake	*	*				*	*	*	*	*	*	*
8 in. front brake			*	*	*							

A7ST Star Twin — Model year

Feature	'51	'52	'53	'54
semi-unit engine	*	*	*	*
plunger frame	*	*	*	*
dualseat option		*	*	*
headlamp cowl			*	*
underslung pilot		*	*	*
offset hubs	*	*	*	*
8 in. front brake	*	*	*	*

A7SS Shooting Star — Model year

Feature	'54	'55	'56	'57	'58	'59	'60	'61	'62
pre-unit engine	*	*	*	*	*	*	*	*	*
swing-arm frame	*	*	*	*	*	*	*	*	*
dualseat	*	*	*	*	*	*	*	*	*
headlamp cowl	*	*	*	*					
nacelle					*	*	*	*	*
underslung pilot	*								
steering lock		*	*	*	*	*	*	*	*
Monobloc		*	*	*	*	*	*	*	*
offset hubs	*	*							
full-width hubs			*	*	*	*	*	*	*
alloy hubs			*	*					
7 in. front brake			*	*					
8 in. front brake	*	*			*	*	*	*	*

A10 Golden Flash

Feature	'50	'51	'52	'53	'54	'55	'56	'57	'58	'59	'60	'61	'62	'63
semi-unit engine	*	*	*	*	*	*	*	*						
pre-unit engine						*	*	*	*	*	*	*	*	*
rigid frame	*	*												
plunger frame	*	*	*	*	*	*	*	*						
swing-arm frame						*	*	*	*	*	*	*	*	*
dualseat option			*	*	*									
dualseat						*	*	*	*	*	*	*	*	*
headlamp cowl				*	*	*	*	*						
nacelle										*	*	*	*	*
underslung pilot			*	*	*									
steering lock							*	*	*	*	*	*	*	*
Monobloc							*	*	*	*	*	*	*	*
offset hubs	*	*	*	*	*	*	*							
full-width hubs							*	*	*	*	*	*	*	*
alloy hubs							*	*						
7 in. front brake							*	*						
8 in. front brake	*	*	*	*	*	*	*	*	*	*	*	*	*	*

A10RS Rocket Scrambler and A10S Spitfire

Feature	'58	'59	'60	'61	'62	'63
pre-unit engine	*	*	*	*	*	*
rocker box covers	*	*	*	*	*	*
swing-arm frame	*	*	*	*	*	*
dualseat	*	*	*	*	*	*
Monobloc	*	*	*	*	*	*
A10RS	*	*				
A10S			*	*	*	*

A10RGS Rocket Gold Star

Feature	'62	'63
pre-unit engine	*	*
swing-arm frame	*	*
8 in. front brake	*	*
190 mm front brake	*	*

A10 SF Super Flash

Feature	'53	'54
semi-unit engine	*	*
plunger frame	*	*
dualseat	*	*

A10 Road and Super Rocket

Feature	'54	'55	'56	'57	'58	'59	'60	'61	'62	'63
A10RR	*	*	*	*						
A10SR					*	*	*	*	*	*
TT carb	*	*	*	*						
full-width hubs			*	*	*	*	*	*	*	*
alloy hubs			*	*						
8 in. front brake	*	*			*	*	*	*	*	*
nacelle					*	*	*	*	*	*

Unit twins
A50 Star and A50R Royal Star

Feature	'62	'63	'64	'65	'66	'67	'68	'69	'70
nacelle	*	*	*	*					
full-width hubs	*	*	*	*					
7 in. brakes	*	*	*						

8 in. front brake			*	*	*	*	*	*
full-width tls front brake							*	*
18 in. wheels	*	*	*	*				
19 in. wheels					*			
19 in. front/18 in. rear wheels						*	*	*	*
exhaust pipe tie					*	*	*	*	*
rear wheel speedo drive					*	*	*	*	*
12 volt electrics					*	*	*	*	*
finned rocker box lid						*	*	*	*
rotor access cover						*	*	*	*
Monobloc	*	*	*	*	*	*			
Concentric							*	*	*
split end forks	*	*	*	*					
oil pressure switch								*	*

A50CC Cyclone Competition and A65SH Spitfire Hornet

Feature	Model year	
	'64	'65
twin Monoblocs	*	*
no lights	*	*
offset hubs	*	*
waist-level open pipes	*	*
small fuel tank	*	*

A50C Cyclone Road

Feature	Model year
	'65
twin Monoblocs	*
small headlight	*
offset hubs	*
silencers	*
small fuel tank	*
high handlebars	*

A50C Cyclone and A65L Lightning

Feature	Model year
	'65
separate headlamp	*
offset hubs	*
8 in. front brake	*
twin Monoblocs	*

A50CC Cyclone Clubman and A65LC Lightning Clubman

Feature	Model year
	'65
separate headlamp	*
offset hubs	*
8 in. front brake	*
twin Monoblocs	*
siamesed exhaust	*
humped dualseat	*
190 mm brake option	*
fuel tank options	*
alloy rim option	*
fairing option	*
clip-on option	*

A50W Wasp and A65H Hornet

Feature	Model year	
	'66	'67
twin Monoblocs	*	*
offset hubs	*	*
A50W silencers	*	*
A65H waist-level open pipes	*	*
small fuel tank	*	*
no lights	*	*

A65 Star

Feature	Model year			
	'62	'63	'64	'65
nacelle	*	*	*	*
full-width hubs	*	*	*	*
8 in. front brake	*	*	*	*
18 in. wheels	*	*	*	*
12 volt option			*	*
Monobloc	*	*	*	*
split end forks	*	*	*	*

A65R Rocket

Feature	Model year	
	'64	'65
separate headlamp	*	*
full-width hubs	*	*
8 in. front brake	*	*
18 in. wheels	*	*
Monobloc	*	*

A65T/R Thunderbolt

Feature	Model year
	'64
Monobloc	*
small headlamp	*
offset hubs	*
silencers	*
small fuel tank	*
high handlebars	*

A65L/R Lightning

Feature	Model year	
	'64	'65
twin Monoblocs	*	*
small headlight	*	*
offset hubs	*	*
silencers	*	*
small fuel tank	*	*
high handlebars	*	*

A65T Thunderbolt

Feature	'66	'67	'68	'69	'70	'71	'72
8 in. front brake	*	*	*	*	*	*	*
full-width tls front brake				*	*		
oil in frame						*	*
slimline forks						*	*
conical hubs, tls front						*	*
exhaust pipe tie	*	*	*				
exhaust balance pipe				*	*	*	*
finned rocker box lid		*	*	*	*	*	*
rotor access cover		*	*	*	*	*	*
Monobloc	*	*					
Concentric			*	*	*	*	*
oil pressure switch				*	*	*	*

A65L Lightning

Feature	'66	'67	'68	'69	'70	'71	'72
8 in. front brake	*	*	*	*	*	*	*
full-width tls front brake			*	*	*		
oil in frame						*	*
slimline forks						*	*
conical hubs, tls front						*	*
exhaust pipe tie	*	*	*				
exhaust balance pipe				*	*	*	*
finned rocker box lid		*	*	*	*	*	*
rotor access cover		*	*	*	*	*	*
twin Monoblocs	*	*					
twin Concentrics			*	*	*	*	*
oil pressure switch				*	*	*	*
twin horns				*	*		

A65S Spitfire

Feature	'66	'67	'68
Mk II	*		
Mk III		*	
Mk IV			*
twin GP carbs	*		
twin Concentrics		*	*
190 mm front brake	*	*	
8 in. tls front brake			*
full-width front hub	*	*	*
exhaust pipe tie	*	*	*
finned rocker box lid		*	*
rotor access cover		*	*

A65FS Firebird Scrambler

Feature	'68	'69	'70	'71
twin Concentrics	*	*	*	*
waist-level pipes	*	*	*	*
both pipes on left		*	*	*
silencers	*	*	*	*
small fuel tank	*			
oil in frame				*
slimline forks				*
8 in. tls front brake	*	*	*	*
conical hubs				*
exhaust balance pipe		*	*	*
oil pressure switch		*	*	*

A70L Lightning

Feature	Model year '72
8 in. front brake	*
oil in frame	*
slimline forks	*
conical hubs, tls front	*
exhaust balance pipe	*
finned rocker box lid	*
rotor access cover	*
twin Concentrics	*
oil pressure switch	*

T65 Thunderbolt

Feature	Model year '73
Triumph 649 cc engine	*
oil in frame	*
full-width front hub with tls brake	*
conical rear hub	*

Triples
A75 Rocket 3

Feature	Model year				
	'68	'69	'70	'71	'72
inclined cylinders	*	*	*	*	*
ray gun silencers	*	*	*		
megaphone silencer				*	*
tls front brake	*			*	*
bellcrank tls brake		*	*		
conical hubs				*	*
slimline forks				*	*
turn signals				*	*
5 speeds					*

Colour notes

These model colour notes are included for identification purposes primarily, and are thus outlines rather than full details as found in *BSA Singles Restoration* and *BSA Twin Restoration*. Most of the detail parts will be in black while the wheel rims may be black, chrome plated with painted centres or simply chrome plated. Headlamp shells may be painted or plated, and some mudguards were in light alloy or stainless steel.

The data should assist when viewing a machine, as an incorrect colour indicates either a change of part or a repaint. This may not matter, but it is as well to know.

Beagle K1
1964	Green frame and tank, ivory tank panels, forks, mudguards and rear fork, chrome rims
1965	Royal red and ivory in 1964 pattern

Dandy
1957	Schemes in light green, honey beige, dark lavender and grey
1958–60	Lavender grey or honey beige, option of ivory for frame and forks with maroon mudguards, tank, carrier and apron
1961–62	Options of maroon and ivory or blue and ivory

Bantam
D1
1948–52	Mist green for all painted parts including rims
1953–54	As 1948 with chrome rims, black option
1955–59	As 1953 plus maroon option
1960–63	Tank and mudguards in mist green, red or black with rest of painted parts in black, chrome rims

D3
1954	As D1 in major grey with chrome rims
1955–57	As 1954 plus options in maroon or black

D5
1958	Bayard crimson for all painted parts, chrome rims, option in black

D7
1959	Red tank, mudguards and centre panels, other painted parts in black, chrome rims, option in all-black
1960	As 1959 plus option in blue
1961–65	As 1960 with option of chrome tank panels
1966	de luxe as 1961 in red with chrome tank panels; Silver with tank and centre panels in blue, mudguards in silver

D10
1966–67	Silver as D7 Silver, Supreme in blue and black; Sports in red and black; Bushman in orange and black

D14
1968	Supreme, Sports and Bushman as D10 models

D175
1969–71	Standard as 1966 D7 de luxe in red, blue or black; Bushman as D10B

Scooters
1959–60	Metallic green
1961–65	Options of red or blue as single colours or with cream weathershield

C range
C10 and C11
1945–51	All-black, tank chrome with silver panels
1951–52	C10 with silver tank, C11 with beige tank with blue panels
1953	All-maroon, tank with chrome panels

C11 de luxe
1948–51	As standard with blue tank panels

C10L
1954–57	Two-tone in light and dark green, option of chrome tank panels

C11G
1954–55	All-maroon, tank with chrome panels

C12
1956–58	All-maroon, tank with cream panels, option of all-black, option of chrome tank panels with either colour

B range
B31 and B33
1945–47	All-black, tank chrome with silver panels
1948–51	As 1945 plus options of tank panels in green for B31 and red for B33
1951–52	All-black, with tank green for B31 and red for B33
1953	All-maroon, tank with chrome panels, option of black but tank remaining in maroon
1954–55	As 1953 but without black option
1956–57	All-maroon, tank with chrome panels, option of all-black
1958–59	Oil tank, mudguards and toolbox in almond green for B31 and gunmetal grey for B33 with tank to match and with chrome panels; all-black option also
1960	B33 only as 1958 in Princess grey

B32 and B34
1946–47	All-black, tank chrome with silver panels
1948–51	All-black, tank chrome with green panels for B32 and red ones for B34
1951–52	All-black with tank silver
1953	All-black, tank chrome with silver panels
1954–55	As 1953 with alloy tank for rigid models and as 1953 for swing arm
1956–57	As 1954 with alloy tank

Gold Star
1949–51	All-black, tank chrome with silver panels
1952	All-black with tank silver
1953–63	All-black, tank chrome with silver panels or in alloy; some USA models with red or blue tanks from 1958

M range
M20, M21 and M33
1945–47	All-black with tank silver
1948–51	As 1945 plus option of tank chrome with silver panels
1952	As 1945
1953–55	All-black with tank maroon with chrome panels
1956–63	All-black with tank maroon with cream panels, option of chrome panels

Unit singles
C15
1959–61	Tanks, mudguards, centre panel, toolbox in red or green
1962	As 1959 in red, blue or black
1963–64	As 1959 in red or blue
1965–67	As 1962

C15T and C15S
1959–62	Tank and mudguards in blue
1962–65	Alloy tank and mudguards

SS80
1961	Black and chrome, option of chrome mudguards
1962–63	As 1961 plus option in blue for tanks, toolbox and centre panel
1964	As 1962 in blue only with mudguards in blue or chrome
1965	As 1964 with chrome mudguards as standard

C15 Sportsman
1966	As 1965 SS80

C25 and B25
1967	Orange tanks and side cover, chrome mudguards
1968–69	Blue tanks and side cover, chrome mudguards
1970	As 1968 but black side covers
1971	Grey frame, red tank, mudguards and side covers for B25SS and same with alloy tank for B25T

B40
1961	Tanks, mudguards, centre panel, toolbox in red
1962–63	As 1961 or all-black
1964	As 1961
1965	As 1962

SS90
1962	Tanks, toolbox in red, chrome mudguards
1963–65	As 1962 plus black option

B40E
1964–65	As C15T

B44VE
1966–67	As C15T

B44VR and B44SS

1967	As C25
1968	Red tanks and side cover, chrome mudguards
1969–70	As 1968 but black side covers

B44VS

1967	Alloy tank, chrome mudguards
1968–70	As 1967 with black side covers

B50SS

1971	As B25SS
1972	As 1971 in hi-violet and black frame

B50T

1971	As B25T
1972	As 1971 with black frame

B50MX

1971	Alloy tank, stainless mudguards, grey frame
1972–73	As 1971, black frame

Pre-unit twins

A7

1947–50	All-black or all-red with tank chrome with coloured panels to match
1951	As 1947 in black or with red tank panels
1951–52	All-black with tank silver with red or black panels
1953–55	All-maroon with chrome tank panels
1956–57	As 1953 plus all-black option
1958–59	Princess grey tanks, mudguards and toolbox with chrome tank panels, remainder in black, all-black option
1960–62	As 1958 with red in place of grey, all-black option

A7ST

1949–51	All-black with chrome tank with silver panels
1951–52	All-black with silver tank
1953–54	Two-tone green for all painted parts with chrome tank panels

A7SS

1954–57	Two-tone green for all painted parts with chrome tank panels
1958–62	Green tanks, mudguards and toolbox with chrome tank panels, remainder in black

A10

1950–51	All-black or beige with tank chrome with coloured panels to match
1951–52	All-black or beige including tank
1953–57	All-black or beige with chrome tank panels
1958–59	Black or beige tanks, mudguards and toolbox with chrome tank panels, remainder in black
1960–63	As 1958 plus option in blue

A10SF

1953–54	All-black with chrome mudguards, tank silver or green with chrome side panels

A10RR

1954–57	All-black with chrome mudguards, tank silver or red with chrome side panels

A10SR

1958–59	Red mudguards and petrol tank or silver mudguards, oil tank, toolbox and petrol tank with remainder in black, chrome tank side panels and chrome mudguards for export
1960	As 1958 in royal red with all-black option or in grey for tanks, mudguards and toolbox
1961–63	As 1960 except no black option

A10RGS

1962–63	All-black with chrome mudguards and silver tank with chrome side panels

Unit twins

A50

1962–65	All-black with tank, mudguards and side covers in green and with chrome tank side panels, all-black option
1966	As 1962 in red, no black option
1967	As 1966 in blue
1968	As 1966 in red
1969–70	As 1966 in blue

A50C, A50CC, A65L and A65LC

1965	All-black with gold side covers and tank with chrome tank side panels, chrome mudguards

A50W

1966–67	All-black with chrome mudguards and blue side covers and petrol tank

A65

1962–65	All-black with tank, mudguards and side covers in blue and with chrome tank side panels, options of red or black in place of blue

A65R

1964–65	All-black with tank and side covers in red, chrome mudguards and tank side panels

A65T

1966	All-black with tank, mudguards and side covers in blue and with chrome tank side panels
1967	As 1966 in black
1968–70	As 1966 in black, chrome mudguards
1971	Grey frame, side covers and air boxes in green, petrol tank in green and white, chrome mudguards

| 1972 | Black frame, side covers, air boxes and petrol tank in bronze, chrome mudguards |

A65L

1966–69	All-black with tank and side covers in red and with chrome tank side panels and mudguards
1970	As 1966 plus option in blue
1971	Grey frame, side covers and air boxes in bronze, petrol tank in bronze or bronze and white, chrome mudguards
1972	Black frame, side covers, air boxes and petrol tank in red, chrome mudguards

A65 Spitfire

| 1966–68 | All-black with side covers and tank in red, chrome mudguards |

A65H

| 1966–67 | All-black with chrome mudguards and red side covers and petrol tank |

A65FS

| 1970 | All-black with tank and side covers in red or blue and with chrome tank side panels and mudguards |
| 1971 | Grey frame, side covers and air boxes in bronze, petrol tank in bronze or bronze and white, chrome mudguards |

A70L

| 1972 | Black frame, side covers, air boxes and petrol tank in red, chrome mudguards |

Triples
A75

1968–70	All-black with tank, mudguards and side covers in red or lime green
1971	Grey frame, red tank and side covers for United Kingdom and grey for export, chrome mudguards
1972	Black frame, burgundy tank and side covers, chrome mudguards

Clubs, spares and data sources

An important aspect of motorcycling is knowing where to get parts and information for your machine. Spares and services are essential to all owners at some time or other, and a list of people and firms who can help can be useful at times of stress. The owner's club can help with this so is well worth joining regardless of where you live. It will provide addresses and contacts which can be just what is needed at times.

To locate the club and dealers, use one or more of the current motorcycle magazines. Hunt around your local newsagent or book shop for titles such as the weekly *Motor Cycle News*, although for a BSA you are likely to be better off with magazines such as *Classic Bike*, *Classic Motor Cycle*, *Classic Mechanics* or *British Bike Magazine*. Within their pages you will find the contact addresses for the BSA, Gold Star and Trident and Rocket Three owner's clubs plus advertisements for services and parts. *Classic Bike* publishes a supplier guide each year in their October issue and this can be a great help as well. The addresses are not included here, and the reason is timeliness. A magazine is printed on a frequent basis and can stay abreast of address changes and the like.

You need to be familiar with these for another reason: magazines respond to changes in the market in a way that is impossible in a book. This is especially important on the matter of prices, which are also not included here as they go out of date even faster than names and addresses. You should be using the small ads to check out values and asking levels well before you go out to shop. This is the way to get good value. Make full use of the magazines in this way as well as for tracking down things you need.

Data sources

Information sources include books, parts lists and manuals. The BSA owner is fortunate in having an ample supply of literature available which does make ownership easier. The books are listed with a note as to the author and publisher, where this is known.

BSA Twins & Triples by Roy Bacon, Osprey

A history of the postwar twins and triples which concentrates on the road machines but includes the scooter and Fury twins. It includes information on the use of the machines in competition, with a special reference to the Maudes Trophy. The detailed appendices are a strong feature and include specifications, engine and frame numbers, colours, prices and carburettor settings.

BSA Twin Restoration by Roy Bacon, Osprey

A guide for restoration and parts identification which thus includes the development history of the twins from 1947 to 1972. The extensive appendices have been highly praised by reviewers. This is the book you need to turn a basket job into a concours winner.

BSA Gold Star & Other Singles by Roy Bacon, Osprey

A history that introduces the marque, with a brief summary up to the 1930s and then in-depth coverage from 1937 to the demise of the firm. It covers the Gold Star and the various pre-unit and unit ranges including the Bantam and scooters. Includes chapters on competition use, both on the circuit and off-road. Has the same detailed appendices as *Twins & Triples*, plus recognition details and a section devoted to the Gold Star alone.

BSA Singles Restoration by Roy Bacon, Osprey

Similar to *Twin Restoration* but covers the many pre-unit ranges, Bantams and unit ranges of singles built from 1945 to 1973. Has the same extensive appendices, many photographs and again, is highly acclaimed by reviewers.

The Story of BSA Motorcycles by Bob Holliday, Patrick Stephens

A full marque history presented as a chronological story with nearly eighty photographs. Covers the history fully.

The Giants of Small Heath by Barry Ryerson, Haynes

An in-depth study of BSA from its earliest days to its downfall. Examines the successes and failures together with an attempt to find the reasons for both. A fine look at what made the company tick rather than for machine detail.

BSA Competition History by Norman Vanhouse, Haynes

A long look at the competition history of the company; mainly devoted to the postwar years and off-road men and machines.

The Gold Star Book, published by Bruce Main-Smith

A compilation of articles, workshop data and parts list combined with a good selection of pictures of the Gold Star in its various pre-unit forms. A very useful reference book.

Goldie by A. Golland, Haynes

Highly detailed recount of the development of the Gold Star with accent on the engine. Limited photographs but a number of line drawings to illustrate the points. The author writes under a pseudonym, but is well known as a long-term BSA technician.

BSA Motorcycles 1935 to 1940, published by Bruce Main-Smith

A booklet first published by *Motor Cycling* and packed with information on the BSA models of the years given. Handy to have.

The First Classic BSA Scene by Bruce Main-Smith

Written, photographed and published in 1980 by Main-Smith in his Scene book series with some 127 pictures in sixty-four pages, all taken of machines as they were in 1980, and all but three of postwar models. Useful reference material.

BSA Gold Star Super Profile by John Gardner, Haynes

Brief history of the one model in usual format for this series, with details of development and competition use plus a photo gallery in colour as well as black and white.

BSA A7 & A10 Twins Super Profile by Owen Wright, Haynes

Brief history of these most popular models, including the sports variants of either capacity.

BSA Bantam Super Profile by Jeff Clew, Haynes

History of this popular model built in large numbers by the factory and one of the best machines for a first restoration.

BSA M20 & M21 Super Profile by Owen Wright, Haynes

Brief history of these old stagers of the British industry that served so well in war and peace.

Triumph Trident Super Profile by Ivor Davies, Haynes

Brief history of the much loved triple which includes the BSA Rocket 3.

BSA Motor Cycles by D. W. Munro, Pearson

Long out of print but one in a series written by the service managers of the firms and bound in red covers. Good coverage from 1931 on and still to be found in various editions at autojumbles.

BSA Twin Motor Cycles by D. W. Munro, Pearson

Another little red book with data from 1946 on into the 1950s.

BSA (Single Cylinder) Motor Cycles by D. W. Munro, Pearson

Yet another little red book dealing with the singles only from 1945 to 1959.

The book of the BSA Twins by W. C. Haycroft, Pitman

Covers the A7 and A10 series with many editions produced into the 1970s, but not as deep or as highly regarded as the Pearson series. Still a handy publication to have on the shelf.

The second book of the BSA Twins by A. G. Lupton, Pitman

Covers the A50 and A65 series in the same manner as the first book by Haycroft.

The book of the 250cc BSA by Arthur Lupton, Pitman

Covers the lightweights of one size built from 1954 in pre-unit and unit forms in the same manner as the Lupton twin books.

The book of the BSA Sunbeam and Triumph Tigress Motor Scooters by John Thorpe, Pitman

Useful coverage of both twin- and single-cylinder models of both marques.

Haynes and Clymer manuals, which cover many of the BSA models in their own special ways. Useful, but make sure that the one you use is relevant to your model.

Thanks to their popularity, most books on the postwar British motorcycle scene contain some reference to BSA to some extent. Some of these books are of a more general nature while others look at specific fields of the sport. Most specialist motorcycle book dealers will be happy to advise on these and their BSA content.

In the early postwar era, BSA issued a comprehensive rider's handbook which covered most of the work that a homeowner could reasonably expect to do. This normally went down to crankcase level and for anything else the firm produced Service Sheets. These covered specific items and were bound in sets to suit particular machines or ranges with many sheets common to several sets. Later on came factory manuals in the modern style either bound as books or in a loose-leaf ring binder file. Many are still to be found at autojumbles or swop meets but if not, there are reprints available.

Parts lists for the postwar era began as one book for each year from 1946 to 1949. For 1950 there was a supplement which was nearly as fat as the 1949 list, but by then the trend was to separate lists for each model range. These could cover one or more years and might again split to cover sections of the range. Thus the first Gold Star models up to 1953 were included in the B range parts list, but for 1954 had their own book plus a supplement.

This continued with one parts list covering more than one year in many cases, and the book may have the start engine and frame numbers on the cover but not always. Often the BSA lists were produced in more than one edition, and altered parts that would interchange would be listed under their new part number and not recorded under the old. This can make their use awkward. By the late 1960s, however, matters were easier with one book for each range or model for each year, in most cases. Originals or photocopies of most parts lists can be obtained. Check the adverts in the magazines and you will soon locate what you need.